Perspectives
for the Future:
Social Work
Practice in
the '80s

PERSPECTIVES FOR THE FUTURE: SOCIAL WORK PRACTICE IN THE '80s

Sixth NASW Symposium

Selected Papers
Sixth NASW Professional Symposium on Social Work
November 14–17, 1979, San Antonio, Texas

Kay Dea, Editor

National Association of Social Workers, Inc.
1425 H Street, N.W.
Washington, D.C. 20005

Designed by Ner Beck

International Standard Book No.: 0-87101-089-5
Library of Congress Catalog Card No.: 80-83988
NASW Publications No.: CBO-089-C
Printed in U.S.A. ³

Professional Symposium Planning Committee

Positions are those held at the time of the symposium (November 1979)

SHANTI KHINDUKA (*chairperson*), Dean, George Warren Brown School of Social Work, Washington University, St. Louis, Missouri

DONNA JO ABERNETHY, Family Counselor, Family Services, Inc., Winston-Salem, North Carolina

ARTHUR F. DAWES III, Social Worker, Catholic Charities, San Antonio, Texas

KAY DEA, Professor, Graduate School of Social Work, University of Utah, Salt Lake City

FRANK FERRO, Associate Chief, Children's Bureau, U.S. Department of Health, Education, and Welfare, Washington, D.C.

BARBARA GRAHAM, Chief of Psychiatric Social Work, Billaview Hospital, San Diego, California

LYNNE M. HEALEY, Assistant Professor, School of Social Work, University of Connecticut, West Hartford

ANNE MINAHAN, Director and Professor, School of Social Work, University of Wisconsin–Madison

FEDERICO SOUFLÉE, JR., Director, Chicano Training Center, Houston, Texas

HENRIETTA WATERS, Associate Professor, School of Social Work, Barry College, Miami, Florida

KENTON WILLIAMS, Regional Administrator for Human Development Services, Boston, Massachusetts

LEILA WHITING (*staff*), Staff Associate, National Association of Social Workers, Washington, D.C.

Professional Symposium Book Committee

Contributors

Positions are those held at the time of the symposium (November 1979)

DAVID M. AUSTIN, Ph.D., Professor, School of Social Work, University of Texas at Austin

KAREN AUTHIER, MSW, Director of Social Services and Instructor of Psychiatric Social Work, Nebraska Psychiatric Institute, University of Nebraska College of Medicine, Omaha

BERTRAM M. BECK, MSW, General Director, Community Service Society of New York, New York, and Chairman, NASW Commission on the Future of Social Work

JOANN BETTS, MSW, Instructor of Psychiatric Social Work, Nebraska Psychiatric Institute, University of Nebraska College of Medicine, Omaha

WERNER W. BOEHM, DL, MSW, Professor, Graduate School of Social Work, and Director, Center for International and Comparative Social Welfare, Rutgers–The State University, New Brunswick, New Jersey

SHIRLEY COOPER, MS, Child Clinical Services Director, Department of Psychiatry, Mt. Zion Hospital and Medical Center, San Francisco, California

CHARLES D. COWGER, DSW, Doctoral Program Coordinator, School of Social Work, University of Illinois, Urbana

JOHN M. DALEY, DSW, Professor and Assistant Dean, School of Social Work, Arizona State University, Tempe

RICHARD L. EDWARDS, MA, Associate Director, Office of Continuing Social Work Education, School of Social Work, University of Tennessee, Knoxville

BEN P. GRANGER, Ph.D., Dean, School of Social Work, University of Tennessee, Knoxville

BRUCE W. GUILLAUME, MSSW, Clinical Social Worker, Child and Family Services of Blount County, Maryville, Tennessee

JACQUELYN HAMPTON, MSW, Administrative Supervisor, Black Adoption Program and Services, Kansas Children's Service League, Kansas City, Kansas

JILL DONER KAGLE, DSW, Assistant Professor, School of Social Work, University of Illinois, Urbana

ALFRED J. KAHN, DSW, Professor, Columbia University School of Social Work, New York, New York

SHEILA B. KAMERMAN, DSW, Associate Professor, Columbia University School of Social Work, New York, New York

ARTHUR J. KATZ, Ph.D., Professor, School of Social Welfare, University of Kansas, Lawrence

JANE H. PFOUTS, Ph.D., Professor, School of Social Work. University of North Carolina, Chapel Hill

JOHN POERTNER, DSW, Assistant Professor, Lincoln College, Lincoln, Illinois

JOYE S. PURSELL, MSW, Clinical Social Worker, Duke University Medical Center, Durham, North Carolina

CHARLES A. RAPP, MSW, Research Associate, School of Social Work, University of Illinois, Urbana

SUSAN SALLADAY, Ph.D., Assistant Professor of Biomedical Ethics, Nebraska Psychiatric Institute, University of Nebraska College of Medicine, Omaha

JAMES D. SHERRETS, JD, Attorney-at-Law, Omaha, Nebraska

CAROLYN KOTT WASHBURNE, MSW, Associate in Family Development, Region V Child Abuse and Neglect Resource Center, School of Social Welfare, University of Wisconsin–Milwaukee

MILTON WITTMAN, DSW, Social Work Consultant, and former Chief, Social Work Education Branch, National Institute of Mental Health, Rockville, Maryland

Contents

Editor's Preface

In 1967, Daniel Bell wrote:

> ... the world of the year 2000 has already arrived, for in the decisions we make now, in the way we design our environment and thus sketch the lines of constraints, the future is committed. Just as the gridiron pattern of city streets in the nineteenth century shaped the linear growth of cities in the twentieth, so the new networks of radial highways, the location of new towns, the reordering of graduate school curricula, the decision to create or not to create a computer utility as a single system, and the like will frame the tectonics of the twenty-first century.[1]

The 1979 Symposium Planning Committee selected the theme "Social Work Practice: Directions for the 1980s" to promote increased awareness of the societal forces to which the profession must respond during the next decade. Chief among these forces are the value dilemmas and changing social needs that accompany technological advancements; the politics of competition in a period of economic decline, the public's tax revolt, and inflation; and the continued struggle to achieve equality for minority groups and women.

The articles in this volume address some of the value dilemmas, changing social needs, and emerging technologies that are expected to characterize social work practice during the 1980s. They articulate new developments and trends in practice, critical issues in social policy, and the dynamics of change in society. Of necessity, they are illustrative. It is difficult to predict with accuracy the many forces that may have an impact on the profession during the 1980s, and space constraints make it impossible to include in one volume all the papers and issues presented at the symposium.

The profession is challenged to direct continued attention to the social problems and human needs that have emerged over the past

---

[1] Daniel Bell, "The Year 2000: The Trajectory of an Idea," *Daedalus,* 96 (Summer 1967), p. 639.

decade. Although this volume does not direct attention specifically to issues such as welfare reform, abortion, the Equal Rights Amendment, gay rights, the needs of the aged and disabled, computer surveillance, energy development, and ecological planning, the profession has a responsibility to assure that issues in these and other areas are resolved with policies and programs which protect human dignity and the rights of all groups in society.

Appreciation is expressed to the Symposium Planning Committee and to the many individuals who presented professional papers at the symposium. Their contributions to the profession made this volume possible. The work of the Symposium Book Committee in reviewing and selecting the articles in this volume and in developing the format through which they are presented is acknowledged. Appreciation is expressed to Frank Ferro, John W. Hanks, Elaine Pinderhughes, and Donald C. Williams for their service on the committee.

Most significant in the production of this book has been the work of Mrs. Beatrice N. Saunders, director of the Department of Publications, National Association of Social Workers. Without her direction, the excellent editorial work of Richard Langstaff, and the support of the publications staff of NASW, this book would not have been possible. We appreciate the consultation and assistance they provided to make this book a reality.

—KAY DEA

Salt Lake City, Utah
August 1980

Part One
CHANGING CONTEXTS
OF PRACTICE

1

Personal Social Services and the Future of Social Work

Alfred J. Kahn and
Sheila B. Kamerman

There is no standardized, fully objective, validated way to assess the state of the social work profession. Certainly one might follow the crowd and consider what can be quantified: the number of members of the National Association of Social Workers (NASW), the totals of undergraduate and graduate social work programs and the growing numbers of their graduates, the jobs called "social work" in Bureau of Labor Statistics surveys, and the projected social work positions in job-market analyses; or the number of social workers who attend symposia, conferences, and continuing education courses and participate in tours to foreign countries sponsored by professional associations; or the entry of commercial organizations into the social work journal, newsletter, and book markets. The authors will not debate those who cite such quantitative indicators of the success of the social work enterprise or even those who count the significant number of clients of social work private practitioners as proof not only of the profession's success, but also of its relevance, while reporting simultaneously the frequency with which social workers are among those testifying before the Congress and serving on prestigious advisory groups, task forces, and commissions. These are, after all, common forms of assessment, akin to judgments about the larger society based on reports of growth in the gross national product (GNP).

Such approaches have their limitations, as social workers are the first to say when they look at other domains. To rely only on GNP growth rates is to push aside questions about the quality of life. Social workers are clear about the limitations of looking only at gross indicators to assess the state of the economy, the polity, or city environments and services. Such indicators are hardly definitive ways, either, of assessing the health of the social work profession.

An alternative approach is to try to estimate the contributions of social work to the society at large. This means not just measuring the efficacy of practice with individual clients, but identifying and assessing the kind of job the profession is doing overall and determining whether it is worthwhile. However, as soon as social workers attempt to specify what we do, why, where, and how we do it—let alone how well and with what response—we, as a profession, find ourselves in difficulty. The going gets tough, and we cannot travel far.

Regardless of what the numbers add up to, the best one can say about social work today is that the profession is "doing better but feeling worse." Yet, certainly, what, why, where, how well, and with what results are appropriate questions and in a good social work tradition. Indeed, these questions must be dealt with as a life and death matter if American social work is to survive.

The thesis of this article is that American social work can continue as a unified profession despite current concerns, but only if it confronts the problem that these queries raise. The cause is lost if the profession ignores the underlying questions: *Is there today a unique mission for social work? Is there a core domain for social work practice in all its diversity?*

Profession in Disarray

The profession is in intellectual and educational disarray. Twenty-four years after NASW "unified" social workers, the new editor-in-chief of *Social Work,* in her first statement, reported on the "searching for unity" as a key concern in a profession experiencing increasing specialization and a proliferation of special interest groups.[1]

A major report on specialization was produced by a joint work group from the Council on Social Work Education (CSWE) and the National Association of Social Workers.[2] It endorsed and paraphrased an important statement of the NASW Commission on Practice over a decade ago to the effect that when the target population, problems dealt with, and the characteristics of a specific social institution in which social work practices are all sufficiently distinctive to require special adaptation of the generic core of knowledge and method and to demand, therefore, special skill, then a field of practice must be recognized.[3] But the report does several strange things as well: It seems unable to build on the long tradition of political science and sociology in conceptualizing institutions and thus talks about "economics" while apparently meaning "economy," or perhaps economy plus job system plus income transfer system. More important, the report loses the insight of the late 1960s that in teaching social workers to relate to specific institutions, one should be able to draw on shared knowledge—part of a generic core—about how adaptation and application take place. Nor, in defining specialization as involving a relation to a specific institution, does it speak to the point that specialization is in that case not advanced, but basic. Theory is generic; all practice is specific. To be specific is to be competent, not *more* competent.

Finally, the most incomprehensible, the listing of institutions to which social work relates ignores the institution to which social work relates most: the general or personal social services. The report lists, instead, "Family, Child, and Adult Development" as though that were an institution in the sense of "Health," "Education," or "Justice," and it ignores the consideration that the well-being of individuals and families is or should be the goal of all the institutions listed. Because the family is an institution of central concern, good policy and practice should be family related, whether in health, income transfer, education, justice, or employment programs, as well as in the personal social services. What is critical in this joint NASW/CSWE document is that the service systems in which social workers have primacy and in which they function most, such as child welfare, family welfare, services to the aged, services to youth, community centers, and day programs, are ignored in their institutional statuses, individually and collectively, some twenty years after Wilensky and Lebeaux became required reading in schools of social work and thirty or more years after Witmer introduced the subject in her long-standard text.[4]

This, however, is merely one illustration; several others are offered briefly. The schools, following the lead of federal funding sources, are taking increasing cognizance of fields of practice as organizing units in curriculum planning. For several decades, however, they have also recognized method as defining specialization. The implicit issue of the relationship of method to field of practice has still not been resolved. Nor do the several bodies concerned with the matter confront directly the question practitioners really want addressed: What is an advanced level of practice—to be certified, licensed, "diplomated," or protected? Surely not affiliation to a specific field of practice or a method, nor basic interest in a problem or target population. Thus, the issue is stalemated, despite reports, task forces, and even curriculum reform.

The schools also juggle the composition of social work "tracks" from time to time with no basis for decision except either administrative simplicity or what appears to a given faculty to represent intellectual coherence. Thus there are "direct practice" (casework, groupwork?), administration-management (community organization is often gone, except in name, and policy analysis appears only occasionally), and perhaps research. The authors' school adds "generalist practice," combining direct practice, programming, and administration. But should there not be some meeting between what the profession teaches students to do and what it thinks most social workers can or should actually do—the social work core mission? Is method not to be conceptualized and chosen in relation to task?

There have been efforts in conference and journal symposia to create coherence and to develop organizing principles by inventing "conceptual frameworks" on high levels of abstraction or by settling on research agendas and strategies for enhancing social work research. The rapidity with which these vessels, once floated, sink beneath the waves and their lack of impact on practice and program suggest that free-floating conceptual strategies are no substitutes for guidelines grounded in the real world.

Nor does social work political and social advocacy escape the problem. The various professional representative groups testify and advocate on many sides of the same issues. Since the profession contains a variety of special interest groups that parallel the many categorical federal service programs and because the categorical initiatives are based on conflicting principles and unresolved premises, the social work profession does not speak in a clear voice. The Congress and the executive branch hear many messages and cannot know which are reliable—or valid—representations of the profession as a whole. Nor do social workers as a professional group have a basis for making choices when asked to rank alternatives. The profession has been told that its spokesmen frequently cancel one another out. Behind this is the issue: where and what is the profession's expertise, its sanction, its point of departure? The issue is not one of denying diversity, but of clarifying where and from what perspective the social work profession can speak and claim the right to a hearing as the profession most knowledgeable about some things.

The history, over a seventy-five-year period, is one of increased differentiation within American social welfare. As social work evolved from a lay activity to a volunteer-professional mix to professionalism, its domain of expertise and specialization narrowed. New occupational and professional groups took over parts of the social sector and developed them. In some cases, existing groups asserted their primacy: city planning, corrections, public health, psychology in industry, and income maintenance.

In recent years, this trend toward differentiation has also been paralleled by an extraordinary growth in the number, range, and volume of services in which social work always had primacy. To introduce Gilbert's phrase, there has been a "transformation" of the social services.[5] The Social Security Act now has a special service title and the potentiality for the support of a universal delivery system.[6] The Department of Health, Education and Welfare, now the Department of Health and Human Services, has created a major administrative entity, which parallels its health and income transfer units, to give leadership to the development of service systems—the Office of Human Development Services.

Social work's current crisis of identity derives from its failure to recognize differentiations within American social welfare and the competing claims of other occupational groups. More important, it has failed to acknowledge, state, and implement its own priorities with regard to a transformed domain of general or personal social services. Thus the lack of a coherent point of departure for specialization, conceptualization of method, social action, or education. Thus the crisis of identity. The problem is one of failure to face the question of mission and of domain. It will not be overcome unless these questions are dealt with head on.

Division of Labor in the Human Services

Social work once claimed all of social welfare, or at least the domain was relatively undifferentiated and its boundaries unclear. That was in 1874, and perhaps even 1919. But the evolution of Western welfare states, East European socialist societies, and the developing world has been accompanied by considerable expansion of social programs, and these have, in their own way, developed their knowledge bases, their technologies, and their specialized practitioners at different levels. In the mixed-economy, welfare states of western and northern Europe and North America, scholars learned to recognize the social welfare domain or social sector as comprising programs, benefits, and services available by other than marketplace criteria and as concerning the living standard and life experiences of the entire population. The practice has grown, internationally, of referring to these as "social services." In the United States, the preference has been to use the terms "social welfare programs" or "human services." Now there is a Department of Health and Human Services, which, in one sense, is a redundancy although it omits education.

The subunits under "social services" or "human services" are usually conceptualized as education, health, housing, income maintenance (social insurance, assistance, and related tax benefits), employment (sometimes subsumed under one of the others), and a less clearly described sixth system.

The authors, among others, have argued that in recent decades this sixth system has emerged, developed an identity, expanded in both welfare states and European socialist societies, and begun to seek—through both categorical and integrated approaches—its most congenial structures for service delivery.[7] The British have named this sixth system "the personal social services" and the name has gained some currency. It also has been called "the general social services." Subcomponents are readily identified as family and child welfare, services to the aged, adolescent social services, or such programs as information and referral, vacation camps, family day care, visiting homemakers, congregate meals, community centers, and so forth. Most of the services are "case services," which are available after a diagnostic or related type of evaluation identifies a need of a specific type. Other services included are developmental and socializational in character, and they are available at user initiative or to people of a given age or status. They are at times called public social utilities. They do not require a case evaluator or a diagnostician at the doorway.

Social work is interested in all the "social services," using the term in its international sense. In the early years only medicine and teaching were clearly outside social work's scope. The profession's range of social action remains broad.

During the Nixon years, when the Department of Health, Education and Welfare undertook a push for "services integration," social workers were in the forefront. The profession encouraged multiservice delivery, one-stop centers, and the creation of statewide, umbrella departments of "human services." What social workers failed to notice was that other professionals were coming in from well-defined institutional bases and delivery systems that remained intact regardless of any multiservice coordination, planning, or linkages. The other occupational groups did not believe that service integration excused one from clarity of mission or from responsibility for one's own institution and the development of a delivery system appropriate to that mission. Only social work failed to see that the components for which it had core responsibility could be related to one another coherently at the same time that social work cooperated in efforts toward integration across institutional disciplines.

The lesson relates to the division of labor. Although thirty to thirty-five states have developed umbrella agencies, no two make the same decisions as to what belongs and what doesn't belong.[8] With perhaps two exceptions, they have not attempted to convert the useful process of overall coordinated budgeting, statewide planning, and administration into undifferentiated delivery. What were previously thought of as "social work programs" have been made the ones to be reorganized, rearranged, and integrated in major ways, and although the other occupational groups have often cooperated, their delivery systems have remained intact.

Doctors know that theirs is the guiding discipline in hospitals, outpatient clinics, public health units, and related medical programs. They have a point of view, which is often controversial, about their delivery system. Educators know their roles in elementary and secondary schools and colleges. The legal profession sees itself as based in and critical to the courts. Services related to employment and housing are less clear and definable. Income maintenance is largely conceptualized and researched by economists and political scientists; it is guided by politicians and administrators, and the programs are implemented by clerical-level personnel and administrators.

Whatever social work's attitudes toward the individual systems and no matter how clear the case that each system needs personnel and influence from outside the dominant discipline, there is little questioning the case for a division of labor in the human services. It is too big a "glob" for one delivery system. There are specialized disciplines with unique contributions. Indeed, there are six systems precisely because of the need for specialization and differentiation.

The authors state elsewhere that

Nobody seriously believes that medical, correctional, income maintenance, and child abuse intake—to pick a few examples—can be unified at the case

level and that one generalist can take on continued service and case accountability (now often called "case management") for all of these. Such an approach runs counter to existing political and professional trends and interests, and would in all likelihood be doomed from the start. Moreover, and no
less important, no one worker, faced with the diversity and complexity of
individual needs and requests, could possibly manage the array of knowledge
and technology required across all human services systems.[9]

There are things to be done about system linkages, overall planning,
public administration in the human services, and the authors have
spoken of them elsewhere. Here the spotlight is turned on the too-
little-considered implications for social work of the inevitable division
of labor in the human services and of the significance for social work of
those services clearly outside the major divisions of health-medical care,
education, income maintenance, housing, and employment.

Personal Social Services

As educators are to the schools, lawyers to the courts, and doctors to
the hospitals, social workers are to the personal social services. Of
course, personnel other than social workers are employed in family and
child welfare, aging, adolescent, and other programs. Doctors are a
minority in hospitals, and lawyers a minority in court programs. The
issue, however, is one of the guiding discipline, the knowledge core, the
operational principles, the characteristic interventions.
Social work is the profession of the personal social services. Social
workers also work elsewhere, of course—in schools, courts, hospitals,
for example. Doctors work in schools and children's institutions, and
lawyers in social agencies, but the distinction is between an adjunctive
and a core role, an old social work distinction.
Most social workers work in the personal social services. Over the
past one hundred years, social work has been relegated, and quite
properly relegated, to secondary, adjunctive roles—however valued—in
many social welfare programs. This does not mean that the profession
has lost interest in and cannot speak to the policy and delivery questions. Indeed, social workers are professionally irresponsible and ethi-
cally suspect if we work in other systems, such as prisons, schools,
courts, unions, industries, clinics, hospitals, and so on, and ignore their
policy and delivery questions. Even more important, however, social
work must consider what has evolved for it as a clear primacy in the
personal social services and recognize that unless the profession seizes
the opportunity and faces its implications, social work will be eased out

and become an institutionless profession—the only human service claimant for professional status unable or unwilling to assume responsibility for a social institution, to devise and be accountable for a delivery system. Social work will be the only profession so insecure as to be unable to build on its expertise and lay claim to primacy in some area of policy and delivery.

The social work mission is to play the primary role in the personal social services. This role involves developing policy, designing and staffing delivery systems, helping the individuals whom these programs are designed to serve, advocating and winning support, assuring linkages with other systems, and supporting efforts that maximize service to the consumer. The role also requires moving out from the personal social services to participate in other systems as outposted workers, adjunctive staff, and cooperating personnel, but the assumption is that all activity outside the personal social services remains grounded in the primary domain. The authors submit that the recognition and grasping of this mission in this particular domain is essential to the future health and effectiveness of the social work profession.

Delivery System Options

One significant consequence of the recognition of the personal social services as the sixth social service system, and of identifying social work as its central professional discipline, is the impetus it offers for experimentation with bringing coherence to the delivery system. It is unnecessary to document here the problems in social service delivery that have plagued consumers, practitioners, and public officials for the past several years: fragmentation, discontinuity, proliferation of access services without service depth, inability to define and organize for truly expert specialization, costly administrative overhead, organizations with inadequate assignment of budget components to direct work with clients, and the rest.

Some see the British solution as an appropriate response—an integrated, free-standing, comprehensive social work service, the "personal social services system," joining together such elements as the traditional family and child welfare system, services to the aged and adolescents, community services for the handicapped and the mentally ill and retarded, day treatment, and so on. A local personal social services department—"social work department" in Scotland—is responsible for the one-to-one and one-to-a-family counseling and helping, the concrete and "hard services," and the group day and residential programs.

On the front line are generalist social workers who function across traditional categories.

But American social workers could decide both to seek coherence for the personal social services and to offer something different from the British type of integrated delivery system, which tries to minimize categories. The authors do not see the advocacy of a single integrated delivery system as critical to the acceptance of the personal social services concept. People may want to experiment in the search for the right balance between the specialisms of fields of practice, such as family and child welfare, the aged, and the court work with children and youth, and the implementation of a generalist practice model through a comprehensive, integrated delivery system.

The authors believe that social work needs a delivery system with a generalist core just as medicine does. It is also necessary that the local social services outlet be social work's equivalent of medicine's health maintenance organization (HMO). Many social work groups campaign for HMOs without considering whether the model has implications for the personal social services. Within the model, various solutions are possible. There are alternative role definitions for the individual practitioner and several possible strategies for designing optimum case flow between types of generalists and variously conceptualized specialists or people who are not specialists in the sense of being "advanced," but who nonetheless have tasks that are sufficiently different and are of sufficiently large scale as to keep them from doing anything else.

What is essential is that the public should come to associate social work with personal social services and recognize categorical units and subunits for what they are—differentiated outlets and staffs concentrating on certain problems and technologies, not because social work cannot cope with interest groups or cannot interpret its work, but because the profession has discovered, empirically, that such differentiated outlets and roles have proved better for some things or for some specific reasons, chiefly because they create better services for people who need them.

Educational Implications

Social work education can and should introduce social workers to the personal social services: the legislative base, policy framework, historical heritage, delivery systems, program models, interventive skills, practice roles, experimental frontiers, knowledge base, and the debate. Retaining a sense of the identification of social work with the personal social services and accepting responsibility for these services are essential for all the reasons that are relevant to accountability, creativity, and professional identity. What better case is there for a fundamental course in the core curriculum to be shared by all social work students?

This does not mean that at the direct service level a bachelor's or master's student can experience everything about practice at once. The idea of a field of practice is a useful one. Students learn generic theory, learn generically and abstractly about practice, in methods courses. They need a manageable "lump" for specific learning; that is the field of practice. Work with children, the aging, or youth, work in the medical setting, work with the psychiatrically impaired, and work in industrial settings or in the correctional field are viable units in which students can go from generic theory in the abstract to practice specifics. That is how skills become real. The purpose is not to create a narrow practitioner unable to move from field to field; social workers do move. Rather, people need to learn how to apply abstract theory to the specific case, how to "case" or analyze fields, and how to focus on a problem or target population.

In short, social work students can learn during training both to understand and identify with the personal social services and to master a field of practice. Both are essential. Some students, because of predilection, experience, or background, might choose personal social services as their field of practice, preferring the overview, the systems perspective, the focus on integrated delivery systems. This could be an especially attractive option for people in management, programming, research, or advanced-level practice training, and it is an obvious choice for many interested in policy analysis and planning.

The authors would separate the categorical-generalist question from the question of what is an advanced, higher level of practice. That is a legitimate issue, and it needs debate and experimentation. It is separate from field of practice per se. The authors' view is that a personal social services delivery system should begin with a bias favoring a generalist practitioner working across categories at the doorway and that this should be seen as a complex, advanced job like that of the medical expert in family medicine. Delivery systems might discover empirically how general practice front-line units would need and use specialists, whether in the form of a supplementary function for generalists, as a function of special people on the expert team, in agencies and units to which one refers and from which one purchases services, or in several or all these ways.

Social workers would still learn about the total social sector, and the profession's advocacy would still be broad. Moreover, because access services are a clearly identifiable function of the personal social services, social workers would have a unique vantage point and leverage in policy initiatives and efforts to create linkages across the human services.

However, social work's claim to special expertise would also be more realistic and more clear cut. In personal social services, social work should demand recognition as second to none. This could help the profession's policy work and social action. Social workers could assert and demonstrate centrality in the personal social services and, from this base of experience in the personal social services, give witness to the human condition and the impact of policy in many domains on the people social work serves.

Why Not?

Why, if the case is good, does social work not move quickly in this direction? Why has it not done so in recent years?

There are alternative conceptualizations and strong special interests within the society and within social work. First, there are those who refuse to see social work in any role of institutional primacy. In this view, social work has a residual role—helping people function in other institutions, helping them adapt to and meet their problems. Social services have no independent validity. They exist only if society is unjust or faltering, and they exist only to serve the deviant, the pathological, the inadequate. The authors' reply is offered with evidence and conviction: to fail to recognize that the personal social services are a component of all modern urban industrial societies, capitalist and socialist, is to ignore the nature of the modern world and the relationship of personal social services to the general standard of living. Social revolutions do not eliminate the need for social services. All societies, including the East European, develop more such services, not less, when they can afford to do so. The personal social services are new institutional responses to new needs. They are constructive factors in the enrichment of society. They deserve encouragement, respect, and a devoted core of professionals.

It is easier to argue this thesis than it is to deal with the iron triangle of specialized and fragmented Congressional committees, federal and state bureaucracies, and lay advocacy groups that prefer categorical problem-solving, are not focused on coherence, and are not worried about connections or integration—or about overlapping, inefficiency, and unresponsiveness in the overall system. In fact, the ethic in the United States tends to forego coherent problem-solving, to claim that this is "not the business of government" or that it "interferes with families." However, this ethic also responds in a humane way to severe suffering, so the responses are categorical, and discontinuous.

By now social work is part of this system, admirable in its way, in its concern with new categories of people in need under many labels and many names—the abused, battered, handicapped, disturbed, deprived. But social workers are also often parts of narrowly defined interest groups, service systems, even specific agency programs that become functionally autonomous and preoccupied with their own activities. As a consequence, social workers often forget the larger target and fail to provide an adequate response and, when needed, a holistic response to people, families, consumers, and communities.

People in such categorical systems, as grantees, grantors, specialists, or administrators, become dedicated to their activities and often operate with seriousness, expertise, and accountability. However, there is no way for overly narrow specializations to create equitable, coherent, and integrated delivery systems or wise social policy. Yet it is difficult for professional associations or large national organizations, in their search for constituencies, to risk rocking the boat. It is a categorical world and conflict can be avoided by dealing with things one at a time as though the actions are not interrelated. After all, Congress has voted it this way.

The debate has spread gradually. New concepts have entered the discussion. The American Public Welfare Association has taken a series of policy positions in favor of a coherent, public, free-standing personal social services system.[11] The National Conference on Social Welfare has moved similarly.[12] Governors, state administrators, city and county social service directors, all see the problem and recognize the resource constraints firsthand.

Periodically leaders in the field of services for the aging talk of the need for a general delivery system.[13] NASW has a task force looking at the question. The Child Welfare League and the Family Service Association of America know that they belong together, but have not yet found out how to move. The Council on Social Work Education has yet to act.

The fields of health and community mental health are especially difficult for social work, and they need to be studied and discussed intensively in their relationship to these developments. Much of health care requires medical primacy, but there are activities in primary care that need to be interdisciplinary. Somehow a way must be found to encourage social work outposting to medical settings from the personal social services and to include social workers in a major way in delivery. Outposting is a helpful way to ensure growth in professionals whose mobility depends on a continued relationship to a disciplinary base. If the public health doctor can be outposted to schools and day care, why not social workers to health institutions? And can the profession not find ways to support social workers who work in health settings in their continued identification with the social work profession?

Mental health is even more difficult than health care. It is a field without clear conceptual boundaries or a clear delivery mission; it is sustained by government funding and the power of federal programs, particularly by the importance of educational funding to a variety of professions. Mental health should be seen as a goal and not confused by being defined as a service. In practice, the activities in mental health settings are frequently medical, but they often include personal social services and sometimes education and employment or training.

If social workers were to make progress in the organization of the personal social services as an individually coherent and recognized system, such a system could incorporate some of what are now defined as mental health programs in such social work settings as family and children's agencies, community mental health centers, and the work place. Other mental health programs would be recognized as integral to other systems—medical, employment, school, housing. In short, social workers could still work in mental health, but without negating the notion of personal social services as the point of departure for coherence.

To conclude, there are political and conceptual problems. There are issues to explore empirically, perhaps experimentally. But social services are not doing well, and much of social work is in intellectual disarray. We social workers need to face these facts and to rise to the challenges. We need to consider our mission in concrete terms and to implement it in a domain that is clearly our own.

Will we?

Notes and References

1. Anne Minahan, "Social Work Unity: Yesterday and Today," *Social Work*, 24 (September 1979), pp. 362–363.

2. "Specialization in the Social Work Profession," document 79-310-08 (New York: Council on Social Work Education, 1979). *See also* National Associ-

ation of Social Workers–Council on Social Work Education Task Force on Specialization, "Specialization in the Social Work Profession," *NASW News*, 24 (April 1979), p. 20.

3. National Association of Social Workers Commission on Social Work Practice, Subcommittee on Fields of Practice, "Identifying Fields of Practice in Social Work," *Social Work*, 7 (April 1962), pp. 7–8. For a discussion of the commission's thinking at that time, *see* Alfred J. Kahn, "Social Work Fields of Practice," *Encyclopedia of Social Work* (15th ed.; New York: National Association of Social Workers, 1965), pp. 750–755.

4. Harold L. Wilensky and Charles Lebeaux, *Industrial Society and Social Welfare* (New York: Russell Sage Foundation, 1958); and Helen L. Witmer, *Social Work: An Analysis of a Social Institution* (New York: Rinehart & Co., 1942).

5. Neil Gilbert, "The Transformation of the Social Services," *Social Service Review*, 51 (December 1977), pp. 624–641.

6. Alfred J. Kahn, "New Directions in Social Services," *Public Welfare*, 34 (Spring 1976), pp. 26–32; and Kahn and Sheila B. Kamerman, "The Course of 'Personal Social Services,'" *Public Welfare*, 36 (Summer 1978), pp. 29–42.

7. Alfred J. Kahn and Sheila B. Kamerman, *Social Services in International Perspective* (2d ed.; Piscataway, N.J.: Transaction Press, 1980).

8. Harold Hagen and John E. Hansan, "How the States Put the Program Together," *Public Welfare*, 36 (Summer 1978), pp. 43–47.

9. Alfred J. Kahn and Sheila B. Kamerman, "Services Integration and the Division of Labor." To be published in a forthcoming issue of *Evaluation*.

10. Kahn and Kamerman, "The Course of the 'Personal Social Services.'"

11. For reports on personal social services, child welfare, and aging, *see* "Special Issue on Social Welfare Goals for America's Next Decade," *Journal of the American Public Welfare Association,* (entire issue), 35 (Spring 1977).

12. *The Future of the Social Services in the United States* (Washington, D.C.: National Conference on Social Welfare, 1978). *See also The Future Relationship between Publicly Funded Social Services and Income Support Programs* (Washington, D.C.: National Conference on Social Welfare, 1978).

13. Robert Binstock, "A Policy Agenda on Aging for the 1980's," *The National Journal* (October 1976), p. 1717. *See also* "Social Services for the Aging," *Public Welfare*, 35 (Spring 1977), pp. 37–40.

2

Social Work and the Social Services: A Scenario for the 1980s

David M. Austin

Futurism involves a mixture of crystal-ball gazing and advocacy. It is partly prediction and speculation and partly a process of lobbying for a particular view of the future in an effort to affect the reality of that future. This article presents three sets of predictions and speculations: the first concerns the nature of social services in the future; the second involves the future of social work as an organized profession; and the third deals with the impact of each of these developments on the other.

Any predictions and speculations about the future of social work and social services must also involve assumptions about future conditions in the society. The first such assumption embodied in this article is that the welfare state will continue. The network of tax-supported and voluntary, nongovernmental human service programs, which are at times referred to collectively as "the welfare state," is an established and integral part of all industrial and postindustrial societies including the United States.[1] The continued existence of these programs, including a wide variety of income maintenance programs, is not in doubt. However, the scope, organization, social function, and financing of these programs will continue to be subjects of contentious policy debates at local, state, and national levels.

The financing of human service programs has become predominantly a responsibility of the national government and will continue to be so. The amount of the government's financing of such programs and the definitions of eligibility for these programs will be matters of national economic and political debate.[2] The current pattern of economic growth in the United States, like that in all industrial and postindustrial societies, will not support significant increases in the resources available for any type of human service program except through increasing the levels and forms of taxation.[3]

Another assumption important to the prognostications in this article concerns the steady decrease, during the last two decades, in the importance of political parties in the United States in forming state and federal policies. During the same period, there has been a corresponding increase in the impact of special interest organizations on policy formation.[4] Many special interest groups have mobilized around human service programs. A consequence of this development of special interest and lobbying structures has been a general balancing of political forces. The tendency of these forces to cancel each other out is a major obstacle to significant structural or programmatic changes in the human services.

Individuals' relationships to the general social structure are important factors in shaping their views of human services. In the United States, individual and household identification with larger structures of social organization is mediated through many forms of group or constituency identification. These include not only occupational position and employment status, which have traditionally been considered the key elements in class systems of social stratification. They also include religion, ethnic background, language group, nationality of origin, sex, age, urban or rural residency, political ideology, and disability status.[5] Individuals thus assess human service policy issues not only on the basis of their immediate utility, but also according to their congruity with the policy positions of the constituencies with which the individual or household identifies.

A common concern among all such constituencies is to achieve equity in obtaining financial support under human service programs. Moreover, constituencies that have historically been subject to inequality of treatment and discrimination have mounted vigorous efforts to redress these inequities through changes in the allocation of resources for human service programs. These pressures will continue, and they will continue to fragment financial resources among a wide variety of service programs and, when two or more constituencies insist on program control, will force the duplication of some programs.

A final assumption is that economic and technological forces in American society will continue to create conditions that result in high levels of personal and household stress and that impose short-term and long-term economic dependency. These conditions will continue to be reflected in high levels of need for human service programs. At least over the next decade, the proportion of the total population defined as outside the labor force and as needing special supportive attention will continue to increase, partly as a consequence of demographic trends. In spite of the possible impact of some types of preventive intervention, the aggregate need for human service programs will increase over the next decade.

Future of Social Work

Social work in the 1980s will not experience drastic internal changes such as occurred in the 1960s. The 1980s, however, will involve critical choices among options that are already clearly evident. These choices will be strongly affected by the underlying characteristics of social work as a profession and by two such characteristics in particular: the profession's position within the framework of formal organizations and its status as a major profession, one that actively seeks to shape the conditions of professional practice.

Organizational Profession   There is a long history of social science theorizing about professions and professionalism. Most of this literature assumes a unitary concept of what a profession is and characterizes an occupation as a profession only to the extent that it fits this concept.[6]

For social work, the debate about the definition of "profession" has been considerably more than an academic exercise. The intellectual leaders of social work have sought for more than half a century to fit social work into the definition set forth by Flexner in 1915.[7] This effort has been only partially successful, not primarily because of deficiencies in social work, but because Flexner's definition is based on an inappropriate model.

The concept of profession is not one that has a single form throughout a society. It is a concept that can only be analyzed within the context of a particular sector of a society. In major sectors of society, such as education, justice and corrections, religion, and government, certain occupational specializations have been recognized as having unique sets of functions and responsibilities and their practitioners have been accorded certain forms of special status.

Two distinctly different patterns are evident in the relationship of various professions to society. In some professions, the occupational

activity involves mostly one-to-one relationships between the person
with a problem or need and the individual with the expertise. This has
led to private practice as the core structure for such professions as
medicine, law, and dentistry.

Other professions have developed organizational structures, and the
technical and specialized activities of these professions are primarily
carried out within the framework of formal organizations. This is the
pattern of the organizational profession. The quality and effectiveness
of professional practice in an organizational profession are a function
both of the skills and knowledge of the professional specialist and of
the appropriateness and operational effectiveness of the service organization. It is a premise of this article that social work is, and will
continue to be, an organizational profession.[8]

In organizational professions, fundamental tensions often develop
between the requirements of organizational development and those of
professional practice.[9] The growth of an organization and its ability to
achieve its goals require that the activities of all its participants be
coordinated. Professional practice, in contrast, requires the practitioner
to exercise independence in making judgments and in using resources
to meet the unique requirements of particular situations. Even in organizations that have persons with professional qualifications and experience as administrators, professional autonomy is limited by restric-
tions on organizational resources and by the policy constraints with
which every organization maintains its integrity. However, it is the
organization that mobilizes resources far beyond what any individual
professional could gather.

Major Profession   Major professions are involved in an organized way
in all that affects the outcome of professional practice. Thus, major
professions are involved in policymaking processes affecting the conditions of professional practice, in the development and management of
organizational settings through which professional activities are carried
out, in the provision of services directly to clients or consumers, and in
the conduct of developmental and evaluation research dealing with
professional practice.[10]

To be a major profession, a profession must define all these activities
as within its domain and must deal with them through its educational
structure. This is not to say that any profession has, or should have,
total and exclusive control over all these activities, although there is a
strong tendency for professional associations to assert claims to such
exclusive control. What is essential is that the profession identify all

these elements as being within its scope and that it exert a systematic effort to improve professional competence in each of these areas.

Social work education developed with simultaneous, although not necessarily equal, attention to direct service methods, social policy analysis, program planning, social action, administrative practice, and social research.[11] Without giving up their basic identity as professional social workers, graduates of professional schools have tended to move back and forth among these various components. Although social work has never exercised exclusive control over any of these activities, it has asserted the relevance of professional input to all of them and included all of them in the professional curriculum.

As a major profession, social work encompasses a wide diversity of individuals whose specialized skills and interests nonetheless fit within a common professional tradition. This tradition is not based on social work's dominance of a single practice setting, as is characteristic of educators in elementary and secondary schools; nor is it based on legally enforced control of a particular type of practice, as in the case of medicine. The social work tradition derives its coherence from a mix of elements, including core practice settings; a long-established set of values; a relatively homogeneous pattern of professional education, which constitutes the only recognized path of entry to the profession; and a relatively stable network of professional organizations, including professional school alumni associations and personal linkages among individual professionals.

Future of the Social Services

As an organizational profession, social work will be particularly affected by changes in the organizational system through which social work services are provided. Social work will, in turn, affect those changes in the social services, but before assessing the possible results of this interaction, it is first necessary to predict possible changes in the organization of the social services.

A brief commentary on terminology is necessary at this point. The definition of "social services" has never been satisfactorily resolved in the United States.[12] In this article, "human services" is a broadly inclusive term, much as "social services" is used in England, but even more inclusive. It refers to a wide range of people-serving governmental and nongovernmental programs. "Social services" is used in this article in the general sense in which the English use the term "personal social services."

The major structural and policy developments affecting the social services during the next decade will also affect all human service programs, and the following points apply generally to the human services. Although social services constitute a core organizational context for social work practice, social workers will increasingly be involved in a wide variety of human service programs.

Expanded Government Involvement   By the end of the 1970s, federal, state, county, and municipal tax funds had become the predominant form of financial support throughout the human services. This will continue in the 1980s. The influence of government bodies on planning and program development will also increase in the 1980s. However, the result will not be a monolithic, governmentally controlled welfare state. The division of resources and legal authority among the several levels of the multitiered governmental system in the United States will guarantee diversity and, indeed, continuing confusion and contradiction in many human services areas.[13] Moreover, at each level of government, the fragmentation of policy and administrative authority among various service sectors and among the administrative, legislative, and judicial branches will further increase the diversity of program approaches.

Increased Complexity   During at least the next decade, the organizational and program complexity of the human services will continue to increase. This complexity will follow from several different factors. First, each type of service program will operate with multiple funding sources—federal, state, local, voluntary contributions, and fees.[14] Second, there will be an increase in the categorical limits on funding as special interest constituencies and legislative bodies attempt to target limited resources to specific populations. Third, with the probable exception of income maintenance programs, the movement toward decentralization of administrative responsibility for program operations will continue. This decentralization will result in part from cutbacks at the federal and state levels in funding for administrative and liaison personnel; the cutbacks will be designed to increase allocations for direct service personnel. Decentralization will also be a product of a loss of experience and expertise at federal and state levels, which may occur as a result of repeated administrative reorganizations. Fourth, regardless of the source of funding, the provision of services will take place under an increasingly complex mix of governmental, private nonprofit, and proprietary auspices.[15]

Changes in Boundaries   A consequence of the increasing complexity in human service programs will be shifts in the traditional boundaries between program sectors. The rigid boundaries that have separated elementary and secondary education from other types of human service programs will be thoroughly scrambled by the implementation in local school systems of PL 94-142, which deals with the total personal development of children with developmental disabilities.[16] The interaction of income maintenance programs, vocational rehabilitation, unemployment insurance, employment placement, job training, public service employment, and supportive social services in the networks of programs intended to maintain the participation of able-bodied adults in the labor force crosses several traditional program and professional boundaries.[17] The deinstitutionalization of individuals with a wide variety of physical and functional handicaps and a related emphasis on independent living require the mobilization and coordination of an almost infinite array of services, with no traditional framework for defining either organizational or professional responsibility for the core services required.

Further, the need to utilize service resources in a variety of organizations to achieve the operational objectives of major federal and state programs has resulted in the evolution of implementation systems that cut across organizational and professional boundaries. These systems are not formally recognized in legislation, funding arrangements, or organization theory, but they exist, with varying degrees of effectiveness and consistency, in every community and in every service sector.[18] In the social services and in other areas such as medicine and education, new types of self-help, natural care, and volunteer-based treatment programs are changing traditional assumptions about the boundaries between professional and nonprofessional activities. The consequence of these shifting boundaries is to open the door to a wide variety of innovations and experiments, although at the risk of unpredictable outcomes.

Low-income Households   During the 1980s, the major types of tax-supported social services will continue to be targeted primarily to low-income households. This will be partly a result of political pressures from and on behalf of ethnic minority constituencies, which are over-represented among low-income households and neighborhoods. A continuing linkage between low-income and multiproblem households will also tend to keep services concentrated on low-income households even when there is provision for broader eligibility.

Importance of Implementation Until the 1970s, social welfare and many other human services sectors were primarily concerned with policy initiation. By the end of the 1970s, effective implementation rather than dramatic new legislation had become the key issue in all human service areas with the possible exception of health insurance, and even in that case, by the late 1970s much of the debate centered on issues of implementation.

The emphasis on implementation increases the importance of administration in accomplishing program objectives.[19] The experience with administration in the human services and in other parts of the economy provides substantial evidence that neither the rigidity of a closed system, assembly line model nor the diffusion of a participatory model, which attempts to achieve organizational objectives primarily by assembling and balancing the interests of different categories of workers, results in effective program implementation.

The administration of human services is a form of the person-environment problem, which occurs at the interface between people and whatever they confront moment by moment in their lives.[20] It involves simultaneous interactions between an individual needing or receiving service and an organization and between individual service professionals and an administrative structure. As service organization networks and organizational environments become increasingly complex, the use of this person-environment framework both for analyzing program implementation and for guiding administrative practice will become essential in most human service programs.

Increased Social Care Services In the 1980s, technological, economic, and demographic trends will result in an increased role for social care services, which involve the provision of personal care and developmental services to individuals with chronic conditions that limit their ability to maintain themselves.[21] Social care services require a continuity of services and access to a variety of specialized services. Individual practitioners cannot provide such services without the support of a service organization. Social care services also require a high degree of personal responsibility and an ability to make assessments and determine interventions on an individual basis, taking into account factors that cannot be dealt with completely through organizational rules and regulations. These requirements of social care programs are leading to the rapid spread of case management as a specific and specialized form of professional practice in organizations. The concept of the case manager will be central to most noninstitutional programs in the 1980s.

Social Work and Social Services

The impact of social work on the social services in the years ahead could be analyzed in terms of the profession's possible impact on specific program developments, such as the increased availability of third-party payments for social work direct services, an increase in job classifications protected exclusively for social workers, reduced eligibility limitations on services, an increased use of contracts with existing voluntary social service agencies, or perhaps the initiation of a nationwide, comprehensive, publicly administered personal social services system. However, social work does not have the political power necessary to bring about any of these developments single-handedly. Only a coalition of several institutional partners could achieve such objectives.

The impact of social work on the social services will not be a consequence of the success or failure of efforts to achieve such specific objectives. It will be a product of choices the profession will make during the next decade. The choices will center on the alternative directions for the future of social work. These two options are not a choice between change and nonchange; both involve change since, in any case, changes will occur continuously through numerous incremental choices. At issue is the general pattern that the changes will follow.

The first option is to emphasize the overriding importance of professional unity around a single, unique methodological model of social work. This would involve establishing ideological consistency within the profession on social work issues, defining specific boundaries for professional practice that can be defended against encroachment by other groups, strengthening those aspects of professional practice and structure most consistent with the model of a "private-practice" profession, and deemphasizing systematic interaction between the organized profession and the administrative structures that constitute the context of social work practice.

The second option is to acknowledge explicitly a broad diversity of roles, functions, and settings, including private practice; to accept and encourage conflict over professional issues as an essential element in the development of a profession; to acknowledge the complexity and variety of professional practice activities; and to emphasize values and historical continuity as unifying factors rather than precise definitions of boundaries and uniqueness. The second option also involves an explicit acknowledgment that social work is an organizational profession and the assignment of a high priority to the strengthening of relationships between the profession and the organizational settings of practice, particularly in the public sector.

It is possible that the profession will make a series of choices primarily consistent with the first option. If this occurs it would, in effect, be a denial of the premises set forth in this article that social work is an organizational profession and a major profession. Choices consistent with the first option might offer short-run gains in income and status for some members of the profession. The net result, however, would likely be that social work would become only a collection of direct service specializations, all of which would be ancillary components embedded in a variety of host settings, including such traditional social welfare services as child welfare. This collection of specializations would coexist with a substantial private practice component, which would compete with other counseling and psychotherapeutic specializations for a limited number of private payment and third-party reimbursement dollars. Social work education might well fragment into a series of specialized components in the educational programs of other professions such as medicine, education, corrections, city planning, public administration, and gerontology and retain only a network of independent psychotherapy institutes primarily for practitioners in private practice.

The likelihood, however, is that the profession will move in the direction of the second option, which corresponds with the author's preference. If the changes occur in this direction, there will be certain consequences both for the profession and for the human services.

Structured Diversity   The focus in the past was on two extreme models of the profession: a model of generic unity in which every professional activity was defined as a minor variation on a single theme, and an unstructured model of diversity that emphasized an individualistic, inspiration-based, anything-goes approach to defining professional practice. However, the simultaneous pressures today for diversity (categorical programs) and coherence (integrated systems) require the development of a model for the profession that rationalizes a diversity of functions and activities within a common structured framework.

To respond to the organizational context of social work, there must be diversity; to maintain professional coherence, the diversity must be systematically legitimized within the definition of the profession. The National Association of Social Workers' (NASW's) 1979 position paper on specialization addresses the task of formulating a pattern for diversity by organizing the human services along the lines of major institutional systems, such as education, medicine, and corrections.[22] Federal support for professional education in the 1980s is likely to be based on aid to practice in such institutional systems, rather than on across-the-board support of professional education. The specific definitions of the institutional systems identified in the NASW paper and the desirability of creating additional systems—for example, neighborhood and community social and economic development—will probably be debated extensively during the 1980s, but the move to recognize the necessity of identifying particular areas of practice will proceed. There is also a need to recognize the commonality of the various sets of practice functions that cut across such practice areas as administrative practice, policy practice, program planning and development practice, research practice, supervisory practice, and direct service practice. These sets of practice functions are not equivalent to the traditional methods of social work since each set embraces a range of interventions, including one-to-one, group, and intergroup interventions. These categories of practice functions may serve as a secondary dimension of diversity within the profession.

The development of structured diversity in the profession, a diversity that recognizes both organizational systems and categories of practice functions, could result in the development of advanced concentrations in social work education, particularly at the graduate level. There would probably be a high degree of similarity among the graduate schools in the concentrations offered. Since few schools could offer all the possible concentrations, states or regions could develop complementary patterns of curricular concentrations.

NASW could reflect this structured diversity in two ways. The first would be through creating mechanisms for registering or certifying practitioner specialists in areas similar to the concentrations defined by the professional schools. This would require procedures through which both current practitioners and future graduates could achieve recognition as specialists. NASW could also provide assistance for ad hoc groups of specialists in the profession to develop a variety of communication linkages. These linkages could involve various degrees of formality and might be open to persons with similar interests from outside the profession.

A pattern of structured diversity would make it possible for the profession to build systematic linkages with administrators and policymakers and direct service workers in the organizational systems of other service professions—with elementary and secondary school personnel and their state and national associations; with hospital, state hospital, primary health care, and community mental health center personnel and their state and national organizations; with economic development, manpower, community action agency personnel and their state and national elements; and with child welfare, family service, and senior center personnel and their state and national organizations. If social work is to have an impact on the human services in the 1980s, this diversity of relationships between the profession and various organizational systems is essential. It is also essential that any linkages between the profession and these organizational systems involve the full range of social work practitioners, including direct service practitioners and administrative and policy practitioners.

Social Work and Social Care   An explicit consequence of moving in the direction of the second option would be an increased involvement of social work with a wide variety of both institutional and noninstitutional social care programs administered by governmental agencies. As indicated earlier, the size and scope of these programs will increase steadily throughout the 1980s. The shift toward noninstitutional social care creates an ideal context for the application of the social work person-environment paradigm in assessing both individual and group needs and in designing and carrying out interventions. Social workers can be employed at all organizational levels of such programs.

An emphasis on social care involves a sharp break with the therapy-oriented, one-to-one model of professional practice. Social care programs require a continuity of responsibility and access to multiple service resources, both of which require an organizational or multiorganizational framework rather than an individual practitioner. Moreover, the key social work role in social care programs is not that of the provider of direct services. Direct service in such programs involves various forms of assistance with the activities of daily living and these services may be provided by family members or by persons in such family surrogate roles as homemakers, foster parents, practical nurses, case aides, client advocates, and big brothers. Certain cases may involve particular types of remedial, developmental, or rehabilitation services and require specialists, including specialized social work services. However, the key social work role is to develop a service plan, mobilize and link diverse resources, and assist the service user in getting access to and using those services. The relationship between the social worker and the service user is task-focused. This type of work is currently being described as case management and is receiving major attention in all programs providing social care. If social work is to have a major impact on the development of noninstitutional social care services, it will be through this case-management role.

The concepts of social care and case management are also relevant to the needs of multiproblem families or, as Perlman describes them, "buffeted families."[23] These are families that are beset both by a multiplicity of personal and environmental problems, which usually involve several family members, and by a limited ability to cope or to use community resources effectively. Even if one blames the system rather than the victim, these families need help. They need continuity in service relationships and the mobilization and coordination of multiple resources, particularly in times of family crises.

The commitment of social work to social care programs is consistent with the traditional concern of the profession with those least able to help themselves, a concern that goes back to Dorothea Dix in the mid-1800s and her efforts to change the almshouse system. However, the future involvement of social work in social care may also entail important costs for the profession. Social care programs are unlikely ever to be high-prestige programs. Even in medicine, geriatrics has difficulty competing with open-heart surgery for dollars and status. Moreover, social care programs do not have high success or cure rates, and the maintenance of a limited level of independent social functioning may be the only realistic program objective. The basic service criterion in many social care programs is humaneness, a criterion that is difficult to quantify in analyses of cost-effectiveness.

Linkage Functions   Much of the response in the 1970s to the growing complexity of human service programs consisted of efforts to control diverse networks of services by imposing hierarchical management systems, such as the state-level umbrella human service agencies. Another approach was to seek operational coordination by mandating comprehensive planning and review procedures. There were also proposals to combine all social service programs into a single administrative structure at the local level. The reality is that neither traditional models from business or public administration nor comprehensive organizational consolidations are adequate to cope with the situation that will exist in the 1980s and beyond. If there is to be a distinctive contribution by social work to the effectiveness of the human services, it will be through the development of conceptual understanding and the practice competencies required to create nonhierarchical, flexible, network-building systems of multiorganizational operations. Such systems must be user oriented and must assume categorical diversity in services and constant changes in program boundaries and agency structures.

Developing effective implementation systems, and community networks of such systems, requires establishing a number of basic organizational structures and staff positions: (1) accountability centers that are located in core agencies in each implementation system and that have responsibility for leadership in program development, (2) a variety of interorganizational linkage, boundary-spanning, or liaison staff positions both at a program operations level and at a direct services or case-management level, (3) a variety of interorganizational working agreements along program lines, including verbal agreements, written referral agreements, and financial contracts, (4) a unified set of information and referral services to facilitate individual access to services and also to provide up-to-date information on the full range of community resources for all the service personnel in the community network, (5) management information systems to cut across agency boundaries and provide accountability information along program lines, (6) a variety of public input and consumer complaint channels to maintain accountability pressures on implementation systems, and (7) formal, community-sanctioned open-to-the-public procedures to resolve interorganizational conflicts through negotiation or arbitration. An important characteristic of this community network approach to service coordination is that it combines openness to the introduction of innovative, nontraditional forms of service provision with the formalized, rule-regulated programs in traditional agencies, which will continue to provide the majority of services.

Various elements of this community network approach already exist or have been tried in demonstration projects, but there are few, if any, examples yet of a community-wide system. The social work paradigm that deals with both individuals and organizations and with both process and structure provides the perspective that is needed for the systematic development of community network approaches. However, if social work is to have a leadership role in these developments, there must be a significant mobilization of resources in both professional education and through the professional association.

Social Work–Social Reform   Social work has always prided itself on its commitment as a profession to the principles of social justice and to action in behalf of the victims of exploitation and injustice. Causes have been a central element in the ideological tradition of social work. The operational application of this tradition has been largely in the social reform tradition of the Progressive Era, when social work emerged as a profession in the social welfare system. This tradition has meant the adoption of resolutions in favor of sweeping social change at nearly every professional meeting and the support of lobbying in favor of progressive legislation. Since the 1960s, there has been a general presumption that social reform means enacting appropriate federal legislation—welfare reform, health insurance, the Equal Rights Amendment, community mental health legislation. Another dimension of the social work–social reform thrust that emerged in the 1960s was the mobilization of protest—Saul Alinsky, Welfare Rights, Grey Panthers, patients' rights. The target of protest was usually the "establishment," which often included human service administrative agencies.

However, the 1980s bring a different situation. The impact of social work values on the future development of human services depends primarily on the ability of the organized profession to function as a major, organizational profession within the network of service organizations and to carry fundamental responsibilities for both direct services and administrative and policy tasks. This means accepting responsibility for functioning within the establishment, rather than operating primarily against the establishment. This also means that the value commitments of the profession must be translated directly into the professional education curriculum and into the professional development activities of NASW. The social reform accomplishments of the 1980s will not be the result of agendas of organizational resolutions or legislative lobbying in Washington. The social reform accomplishments of the decade will result from day-to-day performance at all organizational levels of the human services—performances that embody the commitment of social work to social justice and to meeting the needs of those least able to help themselves.

Notes and References

1. Morris Janowitz, *Social Control of the Welfare State* (New York: Elsevier Scientific Publishing Company, 1976).

2. Ibid., Chapter 4.

3. Ibid.

4. Morris Janowitz, *The Last Half-Century: Societal Change and Politics in America* (Chicago: University of Chicago Press, 1978), Chapter 4.

5. Ibid., Chapter 5.

6. *See* Ernest Greenwood, "Attributes of a Profession," *Social Work*, 2 (July 1957), pp. 45–55; William J. Goode, "Community within a Community: The Professions," *American Sociological Review*, 22 (April 1957), pp. 194–200; Amitai Etzioni, ed., *The Semi-Professions and Their Organization: Teachers, Nurses, Social Workers* (New York: The Free Press, 1969); and Elizabeth Howe, "Public Professions and the Private Model of Professionalism," *Social Work*, 25 (May 1980), pp. 179–191.

7. Abraham Flexner, "Is Social Work a Profession?" *Proceedings of the National Conference of Charities and Correction, 1915* (Chicago: Hildman Printing Co., 1915), p. 585.

8. For a discussion of dropping altogether the concept of "professionalism" in connection with social work, *see* Irwin Epstein and Kayla Conrad, "The Empirical Limits of Social Work Professionalization" in Rosemary C. Sarri and Yeheskel Hasenfeld, eds., *The Management of Human Services* (New York: Columbia University Press, 1978), pp. 163–183.

9. *See* W. Richard Scott, "Professional Employees in a Bureaucratic Structure: Social Work," in Etzioni, op. cit., pp. 82–140; Harold H. Weissman, *Overcoming Mismanagement in the Human Service Professions* (San Francisco: Jossey-Bass Publishers, 1973); and Robert Pruger, "The Good Bureaucrat," *Social Work*, 18 (July 1973), pp. 26–32.

10. *See* Neil Gilbert and Harry Specht, "The Incomplete Profession," *Social Work*, 19 (November 1974), pp. 665–674.

11. *The Comprehensive Report of the Curriculum Study* (New York: Council on Social Work Education, 1959).

12. For another discussion of the issue of terminology, *see* Alfred J. Kahn, *Social Policy and Social Services* (New York: Random House, 1973), pp. 11–34.

13. David M. Austin, *Human Services Planning at State and Local Levels: The Design of Planning Networks* (Austin, Texas: Center for Social Work Research, University of Texas at Austin, 1976).

14. For a discussion of resource mobilization in situations of multiple-source funding, *see* David O. Porter and David C. Warner, "Organizations and Implementation Structures," "Discussion Paper Series" (Berlin, West Germany: International Institute of Management, 1979). (Mimeographed.)

15. "Report of a Committee on Public/Private Roles in the Delivery of Social Services" (Washington, D.C.: American Public Welfare Association, 1978) (photocopied); and "Final Report: The Future Relationship between Publicly Funded Social Services and Income Support Programs" (Washington, D.C.: National Conference on Social Welfare, 1979).

16. Robert Constable and Marguerite Teifenthal, eds., *The School Social Workers and the Handicapped Child: Making P.L. 94-142 Work* (Dekalb, Ill.: Illinois Regional Resource Center, Northern Illinois University, 1979).

17. Benny Hjern and David O. Porter, "Implementation Structure: A New

Unit of Administrative Analysis." Paper presented at the Annual Meeting of the American Political Science Association, Washington, D.C., August 1979.

18. Ibid.

19. Sarri and Hasenfeld, op. cit.

20. William E. Gordon and Margaret L. Schutz, "A Natural Basis for Social Work Specializations," *Social Work*, 22 (September 1977), pp. 422–426.

21. Robert Morris, "Caring for vs. Caring about People," *Social Work*, 22 (September 1977), pp. 353–359.

22. National Association of Social Workers–Council on Social Work Education Task Force on Specialization, "Specialization in the Social Work Profession," *NASW News*, 24 (April 1979), p. 20; and Carol H. Meyer, "What Directions for Direct Practice?" *Social Work*, 24 (July 1979), pp. 267–273.

23. Robert Perlman, *Consumers and Social Services* (New York: John Wiley & Sons, 1975), Chapter 3.

3

Social Work
and the Future

Bertram M. Beck

Futurism and the futurists who practice the art of futurism make most planning efforts with which social workers are familiar seem puny. The futurist holds that it is folly to try to plan how a human need or want will be met, how land should be used, or how an organization might be developed without first positing the nature of the society in which the need, land, or organization will exist. So simple a proposition has immediate appeal. Everyone who has tried to do long-range planning knows that the longer the range, the less the utility. Too often, unanticipated circumstances shape events and demand immediate response, making the long-range plan irrelevant. If it were possible to foresee events, practical plans could be made on the basis of such forecasts. It is little wonder that those believed to be able to predict the future have been honored and feared throughout history.

The contemporary futurist relies not on magic, but on a proposition familiar to social workers, namely, that the seeds of tomorrow are in today. Futurists believe that what will occur in the next minute or tomorrow or next year is a function of everything that has occurred throughout history preceding the next minute, tomorrow, or next year. This is similar to the belief shared by most social workers that if one knew enough about the psychic, physical, and social experiences of an individual, one could predict future behavior.

Actually, social workers cannot with scientific accuracy predict the future behavior of groups or individuals; yet they feel sufficient confidence in the probability of accuracy to try to assist courts, parole boards, and hospital discharge boards in making decisions based on estimations of future behavior. Futurists also make no claim for scientific accuracy, but they still see value in trying to develop what they call "scenarios" depicting how the world might look in ten or twenty years. The value of such scenarios for long-range planning is that they permit the development of contingency plans to meet events predicted. Moreover, by systematic observation and the collection of data, it is possible to determine the extent to which events follow scenarios and to correct scenarios as events unfold.

Thus, when the National Association of Social Workers (NASW) wished to plan systematically for the next decades, it employed, as have many other professions, futurists to assist a national commission in making recommendations to the membership concerning the shape of the world to come and social work's role in that world.[1]

The task of describing the world in the year 2000 involves an inventory of power conflicts in our own country and throughout the world. Historical, political, and social analyses are required to predict how such conflicts will play themselves out and how events will affect one another. These analyses need to be carried out against projections of social and scientific developments that might affect the outcomes of particular conflicts. The complexity of such a task makes it plain that the scenarios have as little chance of accurately predicting the world of 2000 as would the friendly neighborhood fortune teller.

Facing that fact, some might argue that the profession of social work would be best advised to forget 2000 and concentrate on its mission in 1980. Although there is an attractive practicality in the here-and-now approach, it does not take into account the fact that the decisions made in 1980 will shape the world of 2000. If the profession wishes to be proactive rather than reactive, it needs a map, however crude, of where the road it travels goes, and it needs to correct that map whenever explorations reveal the profession's assumptions about unexplored terrain to be faulty. The mission of the National Association of Social Workers Commission on the Future of Social Work is to provide the profession with a map that shows, as accurately as possible, where the road on which the profession, the nation, and the world are traveling will lead. Even more important than that map will be the commission's recommendations to NASW about how to systematically assemble data to correct the map. With such data, the organization can plan activities to insure social work a role in shaping the world's future and to serve the profession's objectives in the face of changing social conditions.

The Futurists' Approach

Although futurists are interested in statistical trends, they are not prone to emulate social workers, who often assume that statistical extrapolation is the major means of predicting the future. The futurists are supported in their skepticism by Harris of the Urban Institute who, in a paper prepared for the 1978 National Conference on Social Welfare, reported that a comprehensive analysis of studies addressing "trends in the economy, changing population characteristics, and human service programs' demand and supply patterns" did not permit a prediction concerning trends in human services. Harris noted that "the past can, of course, be addressed quantitatively and those trends will impact future developments. The future will not, however, flow mechanically forward from past trends. . . ."[2] This is precisely the point of the futurist.

It is common to hear references in social work circles to the cutbacks in social welfare expenditures. This is often coupled with the assumption that the trend is inexorable and the observation that social workers should focus on doing more with less and should be held accountable for accomplishing such miracles. In contrast, a futurist's projection based on an analysis of potential conflicts would not assume the persistence of the trend, but might see the mass of poor people who suffer from the cutbacks pitted against the affluent who benefit. Futurists might also take into account the struggle between groups of poor and working-class people for the benefits available. The future might well be determined more by the outcome of such struggles than by a straight-line extrapolation of the statistical trend.

Even more important, the rejection of a supine acceptance of the notion that what is will be opens the way to thinking about social work's role in creating the future. As inflation erodes the quality of life and falls most heavily on the backs of the poor, social workers may seek a role that challenges the economic myth that balancing the federal budget will reduce inflation. The profession may accentuate activities critical of war expenditures, seek allies among organized workers and minorities, or even question the premise that the American economic system must be perpetuated in its present form.

It would be the height of delusion to see social work as a major force in shaping the future. Whatever role the profession elects to play, a likely scenario related to welfare cutbacks and inflation is the development of a conflict that solidifies the power of international cartels, intensifies poverty and racism, and heightens the profession's dilemma

about its role as an instrument of an unjust society. There is little hope
that looking at the future will make the future rosy, but only that such
projections might heighten the profession's awareness of the road we
travel.

To take another example, consider the impact by 2000 of population
trends. Social work's consideration of such trends usually focuses on
the social and economic consequences of providing support for an
increasing number of elderly people who cannot care for themselves.

A more proactive stance is the one suggested by Pifer in the 1978
annual report of the Carnegie Corporation.[3] In reviewing the various
interpretation of the familiar statistics on births and deaths, Pifer's
focus is not on the needs of the elderly, but on the impact the diminished proportion of young people in the society will have on the
young. He quotes one futurist who contends that as smaller cohorts of
children enter the job market in the mid 1980s, the reduced competition for jobs will vastly increase earnings and opportunities. This
scenario predicts that such favored youths will marry earlier, produce
more children, and divorce less and that pathology among the young
will decrease.

Pifer disagrees. He believes that the interest of both men and women
in careers will make unlikely any increase in family formation. He also
foresees young workers stuck in entry level jobs because of rivalry with
older workers born in the World War II baby boom and not retiring
until the end of the century. He predicts that in the latter half of the
1990s, today's children will begin to advance rapidly, but that

> it will be the job of this relatively small group not only to produce the nation's
> cadre of professional administrative and skilled workers, but to provide
> assistance to the 15 to 20 percent of the population of elderly people. . . .[4]

Pifer expects this responsibility to fall most heavily on minority
groups because they have higher birthrates. He states that although in
the opening decades of the next century the number of workers in the
prime age group will be small, a far larger proportion will be black or
Hispanic than is true today. He concludes that

> every child alive today or born in the years just ahead, whether male, female,
> black, white, Hispanic, or otherwise, will be a scarce resource and a precious
> asset as an adult in the early part of the next century. At that time, the
> nation's standard of living, its capacity to defend itself—perhaps its very
> viability as a nation—will be almost wholly dependent on the small contingent
> of men and women who are today's children.[5]

If social work sees such a scenario as the logical consequence of
demographic trends, the profession's concern for the well-being of

children must be made manifest in its attention to experience in the classroom. Almost 50 percent of all youths entering public high school in New York City drop out before graduation. One authority estimates that the rate among Hispanic youths is 75 percent.[6] This pattern is characteristic of the nation's urban centers. Plainly the educational system is failing, and at the heart of the failure are the alienation of the teacher from the student and the lack of resources. If Pifer's analysis is accepted, what is at stake is not only the well-being of a generation and a people, but the well-being of a nation. Racism, from this perspective, is not only a moral abomination, it is the suicide of a society.

The graying of America, therefore, when examined in the context of its impact on the entire population, may lead to policy and practice considerations of a different order from the profession's conventional concern with home care and cost containment. It must lead not only to a proactive concern for the nurture of today's youth, but also to a rethinking of the profession's view of health maintenance. Much of the concern about the older adult springs from the knowledge that the older one becomes, the more likely one is to experience failing health and to need special supporters. It must be asked, however, if physical frailty is a necessary concomitant of age. Can social workers shape a future in which more is done to preserve health and, therefore, less to cure illness?

Katz, a member of the National Association of Social Workers Commission on the Future of Social Work, called attention to the work of Cassel, a leading epidemiologist who, after a lifetime of analysis of epidemiological phenomena, summarized his beliefs in the following remarks:

> A remarkably similar set of social circumstances characterizes people who develop tuberculosis and schizophrenia, become alcoholics, are victims of multiple accidents, or commit suicide. Common to all these people is a marginal status in society. They are individuals who for a variety of reasons . . . have been deprived of meaningful contact.[7]

Cassel indicated that his detailed analysis of clinical and epidemiological findings points to an essentially environmental strategy for prevention. He noted that disease, "with rare exceptions, has not been prevented by finding and treating sick individuals, but by modifying those environmental factors which facilitate its occurrence." Cassel concluded his review saying:

> With advancing knowledge, it is perhaps not too far-reaching to imagine a preventive health service in which professionals are involved . . . in the diagnostic aspects—identifying families and groups at high risk by virtue of

their lack of fit with their social milieu and determining the particular nature and form of the social supports that can and should be strengthened if such people are to be protected from disease outcomes. The intervention actions then could well be undertaken by nonprofessionals, provided that adequate guidance and specific direction were given.

Katz commented on the implications of an emphasis on prevention:

The view of the etiology of health problems herein advanced has major consequences for health policy, since it suggests that the promotion and maintenance of health, the prevention and diminution of disease in *populations* cannot be achieved and improved merely through the provision of more of what we have, that is through better-distributed and more adequately financed health services by existing institutions and professional health workers. This view of health implies fundamental *conceptual* revisions that will alter not only the nature of primary health care services, but will shift the balance of primary responsibility for health maintenance from professionals to lay persons, from technical health-caring institutions such as hospitals and private physicians, to more natural institutions, such as community centers, schools, workplaces and families. . . . Such an emphasis on prevention, health promotion and the regulation of the environment would necessarily involve new forms of cooperation and health involvement by many kinds of community organizations, and thus requires the improvement or change of present mechanisms for formulating health policies.[8]

Using the knowledge base developed by Cassel, the social work profession might respond to the futurists' scenario that predicts strife between the young and the old by ceasing to rely on health insurance plans that fail to emphasize the preservation of health and that support the high-technology treatment industry. The advocacy of centers for individual and family well-being that embody the concepts defined by Katz may better serve the long-term interests of social workers and society than advocacy of third-party payments for social workers. Although third-party payments can be defended as meeting certain needs of clients and social workers, they make social workers party to a system that is not health sustaining and that can, because of its enormous cost, lead to major intergenerational conflict before the end of this century.

Four Scenarios

Thus far, this article has described the work of the futurist and the way in which scenarios that predict the world of tomorrow assist in shaping the present policies of the social work profession. It has also been noted that such scenarios are often, in their original form, far from accurate in predicting what ultimately comes to pass. They can and should be corrected, however, through systematic analyses of trends so that they become increasingly accurate projections of the near future—say, two to five years—even though they invariably remain highly speculative in their projections of development five to ten years hence. This article has also discussed the limitations of simple statistical projections as predictors and, by way of example, has shown how scenarios based on demographic data and social welfare expenditures may actually suggest policy positions for social work that are designed to insure that events predicted with reasonable certainty do not come to pass. The work of the National Association of Social Workers Commission on the Future of Social Work will result in different scenarios describing the world of 2000. Some might describe a world alien to social work goals and values; others, a world more consonant with the profession's purposes. Either is possible, but the profession must strive toward the latter.

To date the commission has developed four scenarios, and they were ably summarized in a recent edition of *NASW News*.[9] The four scenarios were based on two different world views, both of them familiar to futurists—postindustrialism and transformationalism. The notion of the postindustrial world is associated with Kahn and Bell.[10] It describes a meritocracy in which knowledge is king and science and technology are the major forces increasing productivity, providing the means for the solution of social problems, and expanding leisure time for developmental purposes. The transformationalist theme is derived from work done at the Center for the Study of Social Policy at Stanford University in California. This view sees a social and cultural shift now in process that will take society from its present dehumanized, plastic, industrial age to a civilization that prizes conservation, communal goals, and personal development within a communal framework. Symbols of the postindustrial world are the minicomputer, the brain, and an efficient, well-ordered society. Transformationalist symbols are natural foods, solar energy, and the commune.

Two of the scenarios developed by the futurists working with the commission fall within the context of postindustrialism, and the other two assume a transformational context:

> The scenarios envision the 1980s as a time of struggle between the "achievers," or traditionalists, and the "conservers," or nontraditionalists, in a world torn by waning energy resources. The achievers espouse the benefits of rational, scientifically based decision-making, and extoll the virtues of individualism, competition and materialism as the qualities which "made the country great and will guard her superiority." The conservers recognize the finite nature of our fuel and mineral resources and, hence, the need to reduce demand on these resources by curbing unnecessary consumption. "The notion of voluntary simplicity thus [is] translated into an ecological ethic by which human kind [is] viewed as part of the natural system rather than manipulator of it." "Bigger is better" [is] replaced with "small is beautiful."[11]

Scenario 1 sees the achievers as winning out and becoming relatively successful in creating a well-functioning, but somewhat sterile and alienating society. Scenario 2, which is also cast in a postindustrial framework, foresees an Orwellian nightmare. Scenario 3 foresees the faith in technology shattered and the emergence of communal living—a sort of group worker's dream. The flip side of Scenario 3, Scenario 4 anticipates that the adoption of a no-growth policy will heighten conflict and result not in a society which emphasizes neighborly love and embraces the idea that "small is beautiful," but in parochial infighting and social disintegration.

The fifteen regular members of the commission and the twenty corresponding members are now reviewing the scenarios and proposing changes in them so that they can better serve their purpose. That purpose is not to define the future, but to describe some plausible outcomes given discernible trends. In the words of the futurists consulting with the commission, the purpose is "to *raise* questions rather than to answer them, to stimulate discussion rather than limit it."[12]

Working with the scenarios as they are presently constructed, each commission member has completed a paper describing in what direction the social work profession should turn when confronted with the situations described. The ultimate report of the commission, as envisioned by this author, will be a volume that presents for the consideration of NASW's members the final form of the four scenarios, which will include assessments of how the different patterns of events will affect different population groups and different social problems. The report will define possible courses of action for the profession through NASW, and it will recommend that NASW establish a national database collection system to monitor events and elicit the membership's views on appropriate responses to events.

In their present form, the scenarios suggest that consumers and social workers will diverge sharply in their responses to events. In the postindustrial society, knowledge is specialized, and competence certification is demanded. Social work is pressed to define precise interventions that lead to predictable results. In the transformational world, natural helping networks are stressed, and there is little interest in certification because there is little interest in traditional organized services. A major function of social work in such a society is to provide technical assistance to natural leaders.

To many social workers, the transformational world is much to be preferred, yet much of the profession's current resources are devoted to establishing social work's role in postindustrial society. Is there a conflict between the economic interest of social workers and social well-being? This is a provocative question and one of the many difficult ones that need to be elevated to professional consciousness and discussed as the profession enters the last two decades of the twentieth century. Fortunately, it is not the task of the commission to provide answers, but to provoke thoughtful discussion out of which there will emerge a kind of long-range planning that is new to social work and that will assist the profession "to conspire, to shape the world nearer to the heart's desire."

Notes and References

1. The futurists assisting the National Association of Social Workers Commission on the Future of Social Work are Christopher Dede, Ed.D., Associate Professor and Director, Futures Research Program, University of Houston at Clear Lake, Texas, and President, Education Section of the World Futures Society, and Gail Washchuck, M.S., Research Associate at Wakefield Washington Associates, Washington, D.C.

2. Robert Harris, "Trends in Human Services: Factors That Will Shape the Future," Working Paper 1039–1 (Washington, D.C.: The Urban Institute, May 1979), p. 1.

3. Alan Pifer, "Perceptions of Childhood and Youth," Report of the President, Annual Report of the Carnegie Corporation (New York: Carnegie Corporation, 1978), pp. 3–11.

4. Ibid., p. 6.

5. Ibid., p. 7.

6. Personal conversation with Joseph Pacheco, President, Puerto Rican Education Association, New York, May 1979.

7. John Cassel, "The Contribution of the Environment to Host Resistance," *American Journal of Epidemiology*, 104 (April 1976), pp. 107–123.

8. Alfred Katz, "Future Directions in Health Policy," p. 12. Unpublished manuscript, Los Angeles, 1979.

9. "Conservers Battle Achievers in Futurists Scenarios," *NASW News*, 24 (October 1979), pp. 4–5.

10. Herman Kahn, *The Next 2000 Years* (New York: William Morrow and Company, 1976); and Daniel Bell, *The Coming of the Post-Industrial Society* (New York: Basic Books, 1973).

11. "Conservers Battle Achievers in Futurist Scenarios."

12. Christopher Dede and Gail Washchuck, "Success and Failure: Four Alternative Futures for the Year 2000," report prepared for the National Association of Social Workers Commission on the Future of Social Work (Washington, D.C.: National Association of Social Workers, June 1979), p. ii. (Mimeographed.)

4

Directions for Social Work Practice: The Changing Contexts

Arthur J. Katz

Social welfare as an institution and social work as its lead profession exist within and are shaped by a larger cultural and social milieu. Social institutions are functions of macrosociological processes and structures, which include the economic and political systems and the basic value patterns of the society. These three phenomena usually have a significant effect on the context of social work practice. This article explores one theme from each phenomenon to illustrate the connections. Since there is no body of literature on the sociology of social welfare, these observations are not related to any sociological research.

The Economic Context

How do changes in our nation's economy affect social welfare and the practice of social work? The American economy is experiencing the multiple problems of increasing inflation, weakening economic activity, constant threats of recession, unstable stock and commodity markets, and continuously fluctuating but serious unemployment. These problems create a high level of anxiety in all sectors of society. The value of savings, pensions, investments, and "nest eggs" has greatly deteriorated. Two developments are of particular concern to social work. One is the negative effect these economic pressures impose on the family system. It is no longer possible for working-class or middle-class families to maintain reasonable living standards without two full-time income producers. Almost 60 percent of all husband-wife households in the United States have two or more wage earners, one of whom is usually a mother. This is an increase of 25 percent over the last decade. Although the large increase in the number of women entering the labor market is partly a function of women's desire for greater self-fulfillment, the phenomenon is generally attributed to families' critical need for additional incomes.

American society has not yet institutionalized an effective system to serve the need for child and home care that has emerged along with the two-income family. In many societies grandparents or other relatives are the prime source of child care. In some societies, formal support systems are developed by the government. Social work professionals in the United States must consider what implications this cultural lag in providing for children and families has for problem-solving, program development, and policymaking.

The changing economy is also producing a severe cutback in public funds for social services. As of 1980, the funding for the key program in public social services, Title XX, had increased only 8 percent since its inception in 1972. Since the value of the dollar declined dramatically during that period, the actual value of the funds for the program declined by about 60 percent. In 1978, California voters passed Proposition 13, reducing the taxing capacity of local governments and severely limiting their ability to fund public programs. Since then the nation has witnessed a political move toward balanced budgets and tax limitations and an intensification of the society's antiwelfare mood. The attack is directed against services as well as against income maintenance.

As the economy's problems began to threaten profits, business turned to classic remedies—keep wages down and cut public spending to reduce taxes. In 1979, one business leader said that gradualism in national policy toward achieving social goals was a necessary requirement for a good stock market. Other business leaders counseled patience in the pursuit of full employment, national health insurance, and support for the needy. Placing humanitarian values before economic reality, they argued, gives preference to consumption over production and limits the formation of capital for production.

Business has a high stake in what is referred to as "tightening up" the civil services. During the 1970s, the government steadily increased the proportion of social service work it contracted out to the private sector. Since the contracts were typically for a year's services, this policy increased the likelihood that social work employment would be temporary, created uncertain conditions for many permanent workers in the civil services, and reduced the direct spending for social services.

The issues are not new. As governor of California, Ronald Reagan professed to fight what he saw as the big-spending politicians who advocated a welfare state, the welfare bureaucrats whose jobs depended on expanding the welfare system, and the cadres of professional poor who were charged with adopting welfare as a way of life. Richard Nixon espoused that position and was followed in this approach by the fiscally conservative Gerald Ford and the beleaguered Jimmy Carter.

Although the systematic data are incomplete, a comparison of welfare spending by the United States to that of other industrialized democracies turns up an interesting anomaly: although the United States is low both in total tax burden and in public spending for social security, health, and education, it is high in organized protest against such spending.

The tax-burden in the United States is not a heavy one compared to that of other affluent nations hard-pressed by energy shortages, inflation, and high unemployment. In relation to the gross national product—and despite the rising costs of pensions, Medicare, and Medicaid—the United States is in the lowest quarter among the nineteen richest democracies in spending on the entire social security package. Nonetheless, this country is constantly in the throes of a political fuss about taxes and welfare. This society limps along toward the goal of promoting the general welfare complaining all the way. Every affluent democracy receives popular demands for benefits and services that the government does not have the capacity to provide. People universally seem happy to consume government services, but resist paying for them. American society, however, has been particularly slow in learning how to tax, deliver services, and avoid political disruption and polarization.

The fiscal conservatism of the last three administrations has resulted in a significant negative impact on funds for social services. The results can be seen throughout the civil services in hiring freezes, reductions in positions, salary freezes, and increased contracting, all of which affect social work practice. The voluntary sector is facing similar problems. The use of nonprofessional workers in social work positions has begun to undercut salary standards.

During the last five years, the extensive use of contracting by state governments has changed the function of social workers in public agencies from providing direct service to administrating and managing Title XX contracts. Schools of social work are adding administration and management tracks to prepare students for these new functions. Many public agencies have eliminated all direct service functions for social work professionals, except in protective services. Although it is not new to have social workers as supervisors and administrators in the public services, the trend toward the complete elimination of the direct service function is a historical departure. The National Association of Social Workers (NASW) and other national groups have promoted the development of a national public system of personal social services. Eliminating direct service delivery as a core function in public agencies represents a major threat to the success of any such national system. The public social service agency is in danger of being reduced to a pass-through structure for federal funds to agencies in the private sector. This could result in a loss of professional standards in the delivery of social services.

Social service expenditures do not perpetuate inflation. The ever increasing cutbacks of financial support for social programs can have no meaningful effect on the nation's economic woes. Such remedies as hospital cost containment inevitably fall heavily on the social aspects of health care, and hospital social services have already felt the impact of these measures.

The full-fledged depression of the 1930s produced a strong impetus for the development of social work. Professionals from the voluntary sector provided leadership for developing the new public agencies and services. This effort produced a public social service system intimately connected to the income maintenance programs. Today, the income maintenance programs are administered by clerks and computers. Any dramatic increase in income maintenance services during an economic depression would no longer require social workers. Social services would probably not be expanded, but work programs would. Social workers are now completely cut off from income programs, and there is danger that the expanded use of contracting is fostering a similar trend in service programs. People with degrees in business and public administration are competing favorably with social workers for administrative positions in these programs. In direct services, social workers face competition from educational counselors, counseling psychologists, nurse counselors, marriage and family counselors, and human service counselors, among others. Unfortunately, social work clinicians have

split professional ranks, leaving the profession without the unity necessary to fight these competitive developments successfully.

The Political Context

There is a significant connection between the prevailing political ideology and the fate of legislation to fund social programs. The issue of
social welfare engenders intense controversy in both political parties.
The tax structure responds to such ideological pressures and is manip-
ulated by politicians to expand or stifle social programs. The political
ideologies of Presidents Nixon, Ford, and Carter resulted in significant
losses for social programs.

Is it important to social work which political party controls Congress
and the administration? Traditionally, the Democrats are identified
with a concern for the masses of citizens, the urban poor, and the
disadvantaged. The Republicans have the image of fiscal conservatism,
a big-business orientation, and elitism. Liberal leadership is more prone
to support social programs, but conservative Democrats win elections
and then do not fulfill the Democratic party's historical commitment
to liberal ideals.

The nation can expect continuing fiscal conservatism in elected officials and a low priority for social programs. Any national health insurance program that might be enacted is likely to be highly restricted.
Welfare law might be reformed, but with an emphasis on cost containment and workfare. Tight budgetary controls during the first half of
the 1980s will foster cutbacks in social services and mental health. In a
period of high inflation, cutbacks are automatic unless increased
funding is voted.

The political future seems bleak as the country begins the 1980s with
a strong move into the conservative side of the ideological cycle. Little
effective change and few new initiatives are in the offing. Social work
practice may suffer from either a retrenchment or a reorganization.
Those who need services—the vulnerable children, frail elderly, disor-
ganized families, and the mentally disabled and emotionally
disturbed—will feel the effects most, as will other groups that depend
heavily on social service programs. The Nixon, Ford and Carter pres-
idencies created a political context that works against the development
of a national system of personal social services. This nation needs an
institutionalized mechanism to deal effectively with unmet social needs.
Only an aggressive initiative, projected by a strong, liberal political
leader at the national level, can stop the decline in the social services.

NASW knew little about Jimmy Carter when its political action committee endorsed him in 1976. The endorsement was based largely on faith in Walter Mondale. NASW was greatly disappointed as it watched a once strong social service institution continue its deterioration during the Carter administration. Social work leadership continued to disappear from national agencies, and the influence social workers in appointive positions had on public policy weakened.

However, the social work profession must make a significant contribution to political action. The future of social work practice and services to a critical mass of people in need are closely bound to the political context of the nation. The profession must always work in an organized fashion to help elect a liberal president and Congress, people with sympathy, sensitivity, and a commitment to improving the human condition. Social work practice can grow and develop only if national priorities are changed so that domestic human needs take precedence over international struggles for military power.

Value Orientation

A central hypothesis among anthropologists is that value orientations are important in shaping social institutions. Value orientations are views of the world, often implicitly held, which define the meaning of human life or the life situation of people. They are a critical context in which problems are solved and needs are met. Social workers have always been aware of values as important influences in their own professional behavior as well as in clients' behavior. It is not only the actors, means, and conditions that comprise a situation, but also the value orientations of the actors.

One such orientation in current society is of special interest to social work practice: it is "the new narcissism." The heightened political consciousness and turmoil of the 1960s were followed in the 1970s by a retreat to more personal preoccupations. A disenchantment set in with the social or macro approaches to improving one's life. What came to matter were personal goals and psychological self-improvement. This was manifested by exhortations to "get in touch with one's feelings," by a proliferation of mystical movements, and by the wide currency of such notions as "learning how to relate," "overcoming the fear of pleasure," and being "really meaningful." Although these manifestations may be harmless in themselves, presented as a program and decorated with a rhetoric of authenticity, they signify a retreat from politics and a repudiation of history.

Some observers suggest that Americans are fast losing their sense of historical continuity, of belonging to a succession of generations originating in the past and continuing into the future. The contemporary climate is seen as the only relevant one, and this myopia is interpreted as therapeutic. Personal goals are short-term and do not include others. People strive for immediate, momentary, personal well-being and psychic security.

The narcissism that emerged in the 1970s fosters interest in other people only insofar as they are in immediate proximity to oneself, only if they are part of the system that generates direct and quick satisfactions. The human potential movement projects the notion that it is the individual will that is all-powerful and that totally determines one's fate. This often results in intensifying the isolation of the self.

Perhaps this surge of narcissism is a reaction to the dependence individuals feel toward governments, corporations, and other bureaucracies. Despite the attempt to create an illusion of omnipotence, however, narcissism often promotes dependency on others to validate one's self-esteem. The apparent freedom from family ties and other institutional constraints does not produce a freedom to stand alone or to gain satisfaction in the newfound individuality.

The myth of unlimited opportunities is no longer present in American society. For many, a feeling of banality permeates the social order as they talk about annihilating boredom, complain of an inability to feel, seek more vivid experiences, and attempt to revive jaded appetites. The superego is condemned, and the life of the senses is exalted. At the same time, psychological barriers against emotion appear to have become stronger.

Social workers in community mental health centers report growing numbers of clients presenting such complaints as anxiety, depression, vague discontent, general malaise, and a sense of inner emptiness. Psychotherapists, of whom social workers are a major group, are being asked to help in achieving the modern equivalent of salvation, personal fulfillment.

One can also be critical of some therapists' interpretation of the concepts of meaning and love. To define love and meaning solely as the fulfillment of the patient's emotional requirements is a naive oversimplification. Too often the therapist does not even encourage the client to think about subordinating his or her needs and interests to those of others or to some cause or tradition outside the self. The concept of love should also involve self-sacrifice. Meaning should also involve identification with a loyalty higher than oneself. This is the crux of the social work profession. Currently, such notions are seen as sublimation. At times they are also interpreted as oppressive and injurious to personal mental health. If the human potential movement's liberation of people includes freeing them from definitions of love and duty that involve sacrifice and loyalty, that movement is to be seriously questioned. This would result in a definition of mental health that fosters the overthrow of inhibitions and the immediate gratification of impulses.

The fulfillment of individual potential as a therapeutic goal seems to have become an important part of the organizing framework in American culture. It threatens to displace politics as a focus for ideological commitment. Social workers have long labored to work directly with personal problems and then translate them into public issues. Collective grievances today seem to be transformed into personal problems with the hope that they will be amenable to therapeutic intervention at that level. This reversal results in what some call the trivialization of political conflict. In the 1960s, some individuals sought to escape a sense of personal failure in collective action. Those who waited to work on personal growth until after the revolution found that it didn't work.

The issue for social work practice, particularly for clinicians, is to assess the implications of this emerging value orientation. As therapists, social workers encounter many clients who interpret their malaise as a lack of self-fulfillment. Social work has been an important force in the creation and development of the human potential movement. The profession has helped gain acceptance for the movement's central value orientation in community mental health centers, adult education, high schools, colleges, and community centers.

However, the exclusive emphasis on the self is antithetical to the value system of the social work profession. The philosophical issue is to define the "good" in the good life. Can it be measured only in terms of self-fulfillment? Social work has long maintained a goal of helping people fulfill their potential. Can this goal end with the self alone? Are social workers also captives of the irrational American fear of dependency? Is some personal preoccupation with independent functioning leading social workers away from their historical commitment to interdependence? The social work value system has consistently emphasized the concept of interdependence. The profession has always subscribed to John Donne's thesis that no one is an island. The rugged individualist was never the model for the human condition as defined by social work philosophers, who have always balanced independent functioning with a strong emphasis on the relationship and responsibility to the community.

The family is this society's most important collective. In recent decades, the family has undergone critical changes in its meaning to individual members. These changes came in response to an economic system that demanded the life-style of the nuclear family. The importance of the family as a support and growth-producing system for the individual has significantly diminished. The powerful advantages of extended family life have been traded off for a nuclear unit that promises freedom from the responsibility to care for others, freedom from the fear of dependency on us by other family members. In the Chinese extended family, the very young are cared for by the old, young adults contribute to the overall well-being of the total family unit, and the middle-aged care for the feeble aged. The cycle is a natural one and contributes significantly to the well-being of the total society. Care of the feeble aged and the frail elderly in American society is shameful. Most families delegate this function to that marvelously impersonal social invention known as the nursing home or aged care institution.

In a well functioning, pleasant home for the aged in a large city in the People's Republic of China, the author asked why a facility so seemingly pleasant had so many empty beds. The response was that people were accepted only if they had no family to care for them. Families considered it shameful for an elderly member to be cared for by others. When it was suggested that this system created significant hardship and demanded considerable sacrifice on the part of family members, the Chinese respondent agreed, but added that it assured the aged person of a respected role and a meaningful existence to live in the environment of the family. Emotional and social comfort in old age comes from being able to maintain one's accustomed social role. The words "duty," "loyalty," and "responsibility" all crept into the explanation. "That is the way it is," they said, "a family must always care for all its members."

The American value on independence and individualism goes hand in hand with an almost irrational fear of dependency. The fear of becoming dependent is intense among Americans, who are familiar with the fear that others will depend on them. How can a person look forward to a meaningful relationship with a caregiver under those circumstances? Parents want their children to become independent as soon as possible. At times, this push toward independence is founded on a fear of dependency, and this fear is a strong one. It is passed on to succeeding generations. What American society needs now is creative thinking about the development of interdependent systems. Perhaps these systems will have to develop outside the nuclear family and to replace the support that formerly came from the extended family. Perhaps the answer is a societal commitment to reestablish the extended family. Given current scientific efforts to prolong life, the need now is greater than ever before.

The trend toward narcissism, if not checked, may well rob succeeding generations of the critical dimension of social concern. More than any other profession, social work is committed to the dual focus of internal and external forces in explaining behavior and in developing intervention strategies. People no longer live by bread alone; nor do they live by psychology alone. Social work practice in the decade of the 1980s has a significant role to play in helping restore the understanding that the fulfillment of personal, individual human potential is only a means to a greater goal. This goal is a life in which many people count and in which life is judged not only on personal fulfillment, but also on how one has helped others toward that same goal. Social work practice must be geared to that ancient wisdom of Rabbi Maimonides, "If I am not for myself, who is for me? But if I am only for myself, what am I? If not now, when?"

Part Two

PROFESSIONAL ISSUES, SOCIAL PROBLEMS, AND INTERVENTIVE STRATEGIES

5

Setting Objectives in the Human Service Agency

John M. Daley

Requirements that human service agencies be accountable for the manner in which they use the community resources entrusted to them and for the results of their interventions are an accepted part of life for administrators and service personnel. During the mid-1970s the literature debated accountability issues, asking whether professionals and agencies should be accountable, why, for what, to whom, and so on.[1]

This article starts from the premise that human service agencies and professionals will be held accountable, especially by funding sources, for the use of scarce resources and for the outcomes of interventions. Moving beyond the important accountability issues of why, for what, and to whom, this article addresses the question of how a human service organization establishes an accountability system and, in particular, how the vital first step of an accountability system, setting objectives, is accomplished.

In preparation for the presentation of an objective setting model, the article first explores the distinction between goals and objectives and discusses types of objectives. The discussion of the model for setting objectives in the human service agency includes a description of the process involved and an analysis of the responsibilities of the agency board, the executive, middle-level managers, service delivery personnel, clients, consumers, and community persons. The article also identifies the prerequisites for the use of this model, discusses the resources needed for its implementation, and assesses its advantages and limitations. The model draws heavily from the business literature, especially the work on management by objectives (MBO) by Drucker, Raia, Morrisey, and Carroll and Tosi.[2]

Goals and Objectives

Although goals and objectives have some similarity, the distinctions between them are important.[3] Organizational goals are derived from the organizational purposes. Within a human service agency, program goals reflect the program purposes. Statements of purpose provide the continuing philosophical perspective and make explicit the reason for the existence of the organization or program.

Goals describe desired future states. They are broad statements intended to provide a general direction, and they are brief general statements to the community that reflect the agency's interests and identity. Goals are not sufficiently specific to provide guidance for agencies' day-to-day operational decisions; they are long range and frequently do not include an explicit time frame. Goal statements may be formulated in quantitative or qualitative terms and may or may not be attainable. It may or may not be possible to measure their achievement or even to know if a goal is achieved. Examples of goal statements are "enhance social functioning," "improve the quality of casework services to clients," and "improve community mental health." Goals are set at the level of the institution or overall organization, the program level, and the service delivery level.

In contrast, objectives describe desired future states that are the intended results of interventions. Objectives reflect shorter time frames, seldom exceeding one year in the human service field. They typically have an explicit time frame. It is important that the objectives be articulated in quantitative terms because it is necessary to know when objectives are achieved and to measure their achievement. Examples of objective statements are "to reduce the number of suicides in X population to twelve for the year 1981," "to increase the number of casework hours delivered during 1980 by 5 percent during 1981," and "to increase the number of minority board members from five to nine by (date)." Objectives also are set at the institutional, program, and service delivery levels.

Objectives focus on key results—the important products of the professional intervention. As such, the identification of an agency's predicted key results is a vital step in the process of setting objectives and, for an agency, serves a crucial function in its program decisions.[4]

Types of Objectives

Objectives can be classified in a number of ways. Of particular concern to the present article are classifications distinguishing among organizational levels, among stages of program development, and between administrative and service objectives.

Organizational Levels   Objectives can be classified by the level at which they are developed or by the organizational level to which they apply. This article starts with the premise that objectives are appropriately prepared by professionals at each level of the organization. Daley suggests a practice model that might be used by practitioners on each level in developing their own objectives, action plans, and evaluations.[5]

At a minimum, three levels can be identified at which objectives are set: the institutional level (board and executive), the program level (middle management and supervisory), and the service delivery level. As is discussed later in this article, objectives should be formulated for each of these levels in light of the objectives for the organizational levels directly above and below them. In this way, objective setting in the agency insures that each level of the organization is seeking to achieve results that contribute to the outcomes expected for the overall organization.

Program Stages   At any point in time, a program pursues a mixture of objectives related to its current stage of development. During its initiation phase, it seeks to obtain and organize the necessary resources. Then clients are brought in contact with program resources. Finally, the program seeks to improve the client's life situation. Clusters of objectives relate to each of these program stages.[6] Input objectives describe the resources in personnel, knowledge, or facilities needed to operate programs. Examples of input objectives include "to hire two new MSW level caseworkers by (date)," "to have all counselors complete Parent Effectiveness Training (PET) sessions by (date)," "to move into new office space by (date)," or "to have personnel policies approved by board by (date)."

Process objectives describe the desired results in terms of bringing the program's resources in personnel and facilities into contact with specific clients. Process objectives project the composition of the clientele to be served, the number of persons to be seen, or the units of service to be delivered. Familiar examples are "to have the program's caseload reflect the racial composition of the surrounding neighborhood," "to provide three thousand hours of counseling in 1980," or "to close three hundred cases in 1981." The point here is that a process objective articulates an expected result in terms of exposing clients to program resources.

Input and process objectives are valid and needed. However, each agency or program must periodically examine the assumed contributions of input and process objectives to specific improvements in clients' life situations. Does a particular intervention actually reduce the problem? Outcome or client outcome objectives are specific predictions of the way the client's situation is expected to change or improve as the result of professional intervention. Implicit in each intervention is the assertion that "this client will be better off in this predicted way after experiencing this intervention than he or she would be without the service." Client outcome objectives probably are less familiar to professionals. Until and unless professionals can meet this criterion of effectiveness, an agency's accountability system is incomplete. Examples of client outcome objectives are "to raise John's school grades in each course to a B average by the end of next semester," "to keep Mrs. Smith employed in her job until (date)," or "to pass a bond issue that will pay for improvements to the neighborhood schools by (date)."

Administrative and Service Objectives Administrative objectives are results of agency activities that indirectly support or improve the client service component. Examples of administrative objectives are "to have five active or former clients serving on the board by (date)," "for each case, to complete, jointly with the client by the end of the second interview, a written treatment plan for the case record," "to have each worker provide the supervisor with a complete written review of each case every ninety days," or "to have each worker successfully complete twenty-four hours of job-related continuing education each year."

Service objectives describe program processes and client outcomes. These objectives predict the number of service units to be delivered, describe the characteristics of the clients served, or specify the improvements in the clients' life situation. Examples of service objectives are given in the passages on process and client outcomes earlier in this article.

The classifications of administrative and service objectives are not mutually exclusive. Thus, the objective "to raise John's grades in each course to a B level by the end of next semester" is a service objective, describing a client outcome, set at the service delivery level. The classifications are presented here to explicate the complexity of the network of objectives in a human service organization.

To achieve maximum results from setting objectives for organizational and individual accountability, the agency must consciously pursue a formal process of setting objectives. Although some benefits may accrue from the piecemeal use of an objective-oriented accountability model, only a comprehensive approach to setting objectives assures that each element of an organization is working toward the achievement of key results, which in turn contribute to the fulfillment of the ultimate purposes of the organization.

The Model

Each agency sets objectives in light of its own purpose, needs, structure, history, style, personnel, and consumers. Therefore, the following model is suggested for consideration and for adaptation by human service organizations interested in pursuing a systematic process of objective setting.

The model envisions persons at each level of the organization setting objectives for that level. Figure 1 traces the relationships among purposes, goals, and objectives in a typical multilevel, multipurpose agency.

At each organizational level, persons at that level formulate long-range goals, negotiate with other organizational levels to determine specific objectives, intervene, and evaluate the results of their intervention. Table 1 displays the degree of involvement of various actors at each organizational level.

The following discussion of the objective-setting process generally applies to each organizational level. Comments specific to a single level are so identified.

Long-Range Goal Setting Perhaps the element of the model least understood by human service professionals is the setting of long-range goals. Some confuse goals with objectives. Others view the concept of long-range goals with mixed feelings. Benefits are undefined and distant in time. Long-range concerns must compete for the professional's time with real, immediate administrative and service concerns. Harried administrators and service delivery personnel discuss their priorities in terms of the proverbial swamp full of alligators. The setting of long-range goals is viewed as a luxury and receives a low priority. Neverthe-

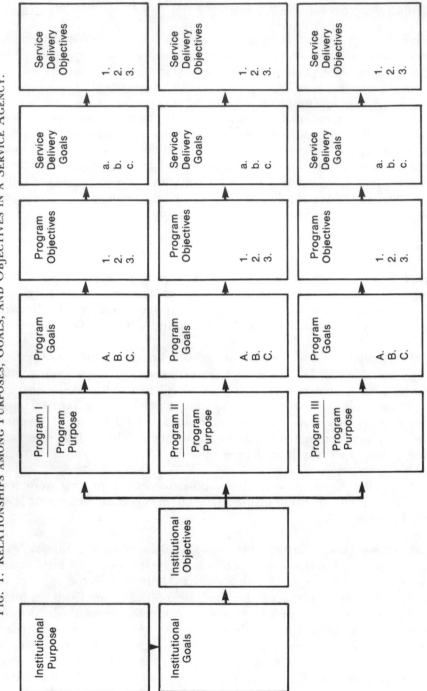

Fig. 1. Relationships among Purposes, Goals, and Objectives in a Service Agency.

less, the present model begins with the setting of goals. Goals provide the parameters for other decisions. Further, they may provide the best opportunities for professionals to establish priorities rather than merely reacting to problems. This is a key, according to Drucker, to obtaining better results from organizational efforts.[7]

In most agencies, the setting of long-range goals at the institutional level needs to be formalized every three to five years. This represents a stepping back from daily operational concerns and issues. Shifts in client populations and long-range trends in society and the community and in professional knowledge and skills are among the circumstances scanned during this phase. The agency seeks to forecast basic trends and to view the agency in light of the role it might or should play in meeting human needs in three to five years. Obviously, forecasts of this nature are risky. It is not possible to foresee all forces in the society or community, and few forces can be seen with the clarity planners would desire. Further, agency professionals are usually not trained or skilled in forecasting.

Intense participation by a broad spectrum of actors insures that the institutional goal-setting process avoids an inadvertent continuation of the existing goals and programs of the agency. A mechanism frequently used by agencies to accomplish this is some form of organizational retreat. The present model suggests an expanded variation of the agency retreat—expanded in the sense that it includes as key contributors persons who are not traditionally included in retreats. Middle managers; service delivery staff; nonprofessional employees, including clerical staff; consumers; and other community persons have substantial contributions to make to the deliberations concerning "images of the future"—the future shape of society and the community and agency's role. A broadly representative retreat planning group can assure that the larger retreat group or "agency family" addresses its task effectively and efficiently.[8] Facilitative techniques and trained group leaders further assure the accomplishment of the necessary tasks.[9] Outside stimulators can provoke the thinking of participants. For example, futurists might discuss what they think the community will be like in five or ten years; faculty members can present their views of knowledge or skill breakthroughs likely to be available to the helping professions; government representatives might discuss changes likely in government involvement in meeting human service needs; or social demographers might describe the community's population of the future. The point here is to help the agency family extend its thinking, imagery, and expectations beyond the present.

Table 1.

Degree of Involvement of Various Actors during Agency Objective-Setting Process

			Actor			
	Board	Executive	Program Managers or Supervisors	Service Delivery Staff	Clients or Consumers	Communities[a]
Institutional level						
Goals	High	High	Medium	Medium	Medium	Medium
Objectives						
Follow-up						
Program level						
Goals	Medium	High	High	Medium	Low[b]	Low[b]
Objectives						
Follow-up						
Service delivery level						
Goals	Low	Medium	Medium	High	High	Low[b]
Objectives						
Follow-up						

[a] Community actors might include elected or appointed community policymakers, representatives of funding sources or other service, planning, or allocating agencies, and so on.

[b] Participation by consumers and other community persons at the program level and by community persons at the service delivery level is accomplished by having clients and community representatives hold board membership.

Once trends are forecasted, however tentatively, the role of the agency in the future can begin to be considered, and the broad outlines of its projected purpose can be drawn. This broad and general description of the projected purposes of the agency, once formulated by the agency family, must be accepted for the agency by its board of directors. Goals may identify future problems to be dealt with, kinds of service methods to be used, populations to be served, personnel to be employed, and so on. Long-range goals are accepted with the recognition that they are based on incomplete knowledge and understanding. The resources devoted to this phase of the process need not approach the level of resources in time or money required for objective setting and follow-up. For example, staff and board members working on the ad hoc retreat planning committee could complete preparations for the retreat within, at most, a two-month or three-month planning process, involving a handful of well-structured meetings. The retreat itself will occupy one or two days for participants. Follow-up activities to bring the results of the retreat to the board form part of the board's regular planning process. Therefore, although specific resources must be invested, the resources necessary are limited.

Short-Range Objectives The long-range goals provide the general direction for the institution, program, or service delivery episode. Within these parameters, short-term objectives, which project for a year or less, indicate in specific terms the predicted results of professional efforts.

It is appropriate to set objectives at each level of the agency. At the top of the agency hierarchy, the board is assisted by the executive in setting objectives. Based on these organizational objectives, program managers and supervisors develop objectives for their components, indicating the key results each component will contribute to the organizational objectives. Service delivery workers in turn indicate in their own objectives the key products they will contribute to their component's results. In each case, the higher organizational authority communicates as directly and clearly as possible its objectives to persons at the next lower organizational level. The persons at the next lower level use the objectives of the higher level to guide the development of their objectives. At each level, negotiations occur as persons at the lower level develop their objectives. Thus, although a general roll-down or cascade effect is present, objectives at any level of the organization may contribute to changes being made in the objectives of higher levels as reactions reverberate back up the organization. Multiple negotiations tie the key results of program components into a system of objectives, using the tension of the roll-down or cascade effect to unify efforts toward achieving organizational purposes.[10]

Intervention and Follow-Up Objectives provide the opportunity for an agency and its components, including individuals, to predict the key results of their efforts. Objectives are building blocks in an account-ability system. The system is not complete when a "final" set of objec-tives has been agreed to by the various actors. Objectives provide one side of the accountability coin. The other side is represented by the actual outcomes. To obtain the benefits of an accountability system, the agency must develop an information system that provides persons at each level of the organization with the data they need to monitor progress toward the accomplishment of objectives. Further, means need to be developed to insure that the timing, format, and content of program-monitoring information make the information usable and that the information is used in the planning, administrative, and evaluative processes of the agency.[11] Based on a review of the agency's experience, adjustments may be made in the objectives, in the resources applied to each objective, or in the strategies to achieve specific objec-tives. These experience-based incremental changes in a program are founded on interim information and provide the manager or profes-sional a high degree of flexibility in program development.

Costs and Benefits of Objective Setting

The costs include the time and other resources needed to implement a systematic process of setting objectives. Considerations of cost must take into account the time lost from other agency activities, the training costs, and the frustrations and resistance encountered in the initiation of any new technological or philosophical system. Finally, setting objec-tives means that failures and weaknesses may be identified and doc-umented. Fears that specifying objectives may be used punitively prob-ably reflect more on the existent managerial philosophy in an agency than on objective setting or MBO as a system.[12]

The benefits of using this model of setting objectives include the advantages traditionally associated with MBO—individual efforts di-rected toward organizational purposes; enhanced motivation of per-sonnel through participation in setting objectives; improved planning and management capabilities, potentially leading to improved pro-gramming; reduced role conflict and ambiguity; identification and consequent rewarding of productive elements of the organization; and the creation of an opportunity to identify and improve unproductive components. Of particular importance to human service agencies are the tangible criteria of appraisal that the objective-setting model provides.[13] The costs of not using an objective-based accountability system must be considered. Frequently, human service programs serve populations that are not highly valued by the general population or by policymakers. An objective-based accountability system offers an agency an insurance policy against possible ideological attacks on programs serving poor or other populations not highly valued by influential elements of the society.

Prerequisites and Resources

Clear and honest communication and a high quality of interaction between agency policymakers and staff, and among staff at various levels of the organization, appear essential to fruitful objective setting.[14] The objective-setting process proposed in this article requires, above all, a commitment by the various actors to this type of accountability system. This action commitment—the willingness to do what is necessary—must be clearly and consistently evidenced by the agency leadership, both board and staff.

The commitment must be based on an informed evaluation by each actor that the investment of resources in the objective-setting process will yield specific benefits to the individual professional and the agency. Therefore, an understanding of the costs and benefits of the process is a prerequisite to commitment.

Time to understand the objective setting process, to learn the requisite skills, and to refine these skills is necessary. A frequent objection to objective setting is the time required to draft articulate and measurable objectives. Frequently overlooked is the time needed to identify the key results of interventions. Initial efforts in these areas can be expected to require time and patience. As skills improve, the process will require less time. During the process of developing objectives and initiating an objective-based accountability system a "disenchantment period" can be expected and should be acknowledged when the costs to various actors are more readily apparent than the benefits. This learning phase will test the commitment of the policymakers and top management as the process cascades down the organization.[15] The point remains, investments must be evaluated in terms of expected benefits.

In summary, this article presents a model for setting objectives in a human service agency, a necessary first step in developing a comprehensive accountability system for the agency. The model requires that an agency invest resources in the process of setting objectives if the benefits of an objective-focused accountability system are to be achieved. Social work agencies must make this investment if they are to retain strong claims on the limited human service resources available in the 1980s.

Notes and References

1. For a review of the literature on the accountability debate, *see* John M. Daley, "Practice By Objectives," in Bernard Ross and Shanti K. Khinduka, eds., *Social Work in Practice* (New York: National Association of Social Workers, 1976), pp. 241–251.

2. Peter F. Drucker, *The Practice of Management* and *Managing for Results* (New York: Harper & Row, 1954 and 1964, respectively), Anthony P. Raia, *Managing by Objectives* (Glenview, Ill.: Scott, Foresman & Co., 1974); George L. Morrisey, *Management by Objectives and Results* (Reading, Mass.: Addison-Wesley Publishing Co., 1970); and Stephen J. Carroll, Jr., and Henry L. Tosi, Jr., *Management by Objectives: Applications and Research* (New York: Macmillan Publishing Co., 1973).

3. Daley, op. cit., pp. 243–244; Raia, op. cit., pp. 23–24, 64–67; Morrisey, op. cit., pp. 52–63; Carroll and Tosi, op. cit., pp. 69–88; Robert F. Mayer, *Preparing Instructional Objectives* (Belmont, Calif.: Fearon, 1962); Ralph Brody and Holly Krailo, "An Approach to Reviewing the Effectiveness of Programs," *Social Work*, 23 (May 1978), pp. 226–232, especially pp. 227–228.

4. On subjectives, which are less tangible results that are unusually difficult or expensive to measure—for example, "to improve communication between administrators and professional staff"—and which are stated in terms of verifiable activities whose successful completion is assumed to lead to the desired results, *see* Morrisey, op. cit., p. 47; and Raia, op. cit., p. 25; and Paul Mali, *Managing by Objectives* (New York: Wiley-Interscience, 1972), p. 116.

5. Daley, op. cit.; *see also*, Raia, op. cit., pp. 11 and 59.

6. For suggestions of classifications similar to input, process, and outcome, *see* Tony Tripodi, Phillip Fellin, and Irwin Epstein, *Differential Social Program Evaluation* (Itasca, Ill.: F. E. Peacock Publishers, 1978), pp. 22–37; and Brody and Krailo, op. cit., p. 227.

7. Drucker, *Managing for Results*, op. cit., pp. 5–6, 131–150, and 173–202.

8. For the terms "images of the future" and "agency family," the author is indebted to Bob Rundell of the Human Resource Center, University of Texas, Arlington.

9. *See*, for example, Andra L. Delbecq, Andrew H. Van de Ven, and David H. Gustafson, *Group Techniques for Program Planning* (Glenview, Ill.: Scott,

Foresman & Co., 1975); and Harold P. Zelko, *Successful Conference and Discussion Techniques* (New York: McGraw-Hill Book Co., 1975); and Harold P. Zelko, *Successful Conference and Discussion Techniques* (New York: McGraw-Hill Book Co., 1957); Morrisey, op. cit., pp. 19–37; and Mali, op. cit., pp. 71–82.

10. For a discussion of multilevel linkage, *see* James D. Thompson, "Common and Uncommon Elements in Administration," in Harry A. Schatz, ed., *Social Work Administration: A Resource Book* (New York: Council on Social Work Education, 1970), pp. 30–42. *See also* W. J. Reddin, *Effective Management by Objectives* (New York: McGraw-Hill Book Co., 1971), pp. 176–179; Raia, op. cit., pp. 29–37 and 57–58; and Mali, op. cit., pp. 22–26, and 127–133.

11. Concerning information systems and the use of feedback to adjust objectives, methods, and resources, *see* Daley, op. cit. For an excellent discussion of ways evaluators can improve the probability that their findings will be used by administrators, *see* Carol H. Weiss, "Utilization of Evaluation: Toward Comparative Study," in Weiss, ed., *Evaluating Action Programs* (Boston: Allyn & Bacon, 1972), pp. 318–326. *See also* Carroll and Tosi, op. cit., pp. 5 and 42; and Morrisey, op. cit., pp. 131–136.

12. Carroll and Tosi, op. cit., pp. 13–15; 49–52; and Raia, op. cit., pp. 148–151.

13. For an extended discussion of the potential advantages of MBO, *see* Carroll and Tosi, op. cit., pp. 129–138. *See also* Mali, op. cit., pp. 57–64.

14. Raia, op. cit., p. 52.

15. Carroll and Tosi, op. cit., pp. 53–56. For a discussion of the advantages and disadvantages of various strategies of implementation of MBO (top down, bottom up, simultaneous), *see* Morrisey, op. cit., pp. 155–160.

6

Public Child Welfare in the 1980s: The Role of Case Management

Charles A. Rapp and John Poertner

Public child welfare workers are becoming case managers. This new model replaces the traditional casework model and emphasizes workers as professional decision-makers. As such they assume, on a case-by-case basis, many functions traditionally reserved for administrators. Although administrators and managers have long been viewed as decision-makers and management tools developed to assist them in their decision-making, comparable tools for public child welfare practitioners have been slow to develop. Studies of caseworker decision-making testify to this fact and also show that workers' decisions vary widely.[1] Workers often avoid making decisions or base them on expediency.[2] The drift of children in foster care has been attributed to delayed and protracted decision-making by caseworkers, parents, and juvenile justice personnel.[3] There is also evidence that decisions are not based on the best available knowledge. Not only do social workers not use knowledge gained from research, but they have a low opinion of research.[4]

Public child welfare workers have not completed the transition to their new case management role, and the profession has not developed the tools to assist them in defining this role. This article seeks to define the case manager role and the criteria for the decision-making that will shape public child welfare in the 1980s.

In the past, the responsibilities of public child welfare workers were similar to those of workers in the private sector. They had relatively small caseloads and delivered services directly. They met with the families, engaged in problem-solving in a wide variety of areas, offered advice and counsel, and, when necessary, placed children. Few services were available other than placement and counseling. The job of public child welfare workers has been changed by a variety of factors, including a politically active voluntary sector, a wider variety of child welfare services, increased mandates, and a hesitance on the part of the public to allow public social service agencies to increase their staffing.

Increasingly, the private sector is looking to the public treasury for funding. United Funds and other private fund-raising organizations cannot raise enough money to keep up with the expanded range of services the private sector is providing. As a result, in states that have long had large and active voluntary sectors, political pressure has been brought to bear to increase public subsidies for services. These subsidies have been provided largely through the mechanism of purchase-of-service contracts. The 1967 Social Security Act amendments accelerated this contracting, and in 1974, Title XX of the Social Security Act contained provisions that further increased the use of purchase-of-service contracts. A recent study conducted by the Urban Institute reported that "purchased services are now the predominant mode of service delivery nationally."[5]

Support for this form of service delivery is not purely political. Commentators on child welfare note that the voluntary sector is more likely than public agencies to attract highly skilled persons, to generate innovations in the delivery of services, to increase local accountability and support for programs, and to tailor programs for a given community.

The expanded range of services provided by child welfare agencies has also affected the role of the workers. Services were traditionally limited to counseling and placement, with counseling usually occurring before, during, and after placement. It is not unusual today to find child welfare agencies providing homemakers, day care, alternative education programs, day treatment programs, vocational training, legal assistance, and advocacy services. The changes have been occurring concurrently with broadening mandates from legislatures and case law.

Child welfare traditionally concerned services for orphans and dependent, neglected, and abused children. It is not uncommon today to find child welfare departments responsible for delinquents, minors in need of supervision, and handicapped and emotionally disturbed children as well as for their traditional clients. The public has also discovered child abuse and neglect and is demanding investigations into an increasingly large number of cases.

A variety of other factors have also contributed to changing the role of the public child welfare worker. Citizen distrust of bureaucracies and large public payrolls have created new kinds of pressures. Public agency staffs have not kept up with the radical increase in child abuse and neglect reports, and as a result, caseloads are large and getting larger. It is not uncommon to find workers with caseloads of sixty or eighty. At the same time, workers have been expected to perform additional duties, such as the recruitment and training of foster families and the coordination of services, and to confront a rapid rise in paperwork. It is this combination of factors that prohibits the traditional modes of delivering child welfare services.

Case Management

Case manager is not some newly created position, but a modification of familiar job descriptions. The case manager is what is now known as the caseworker or direct service worker. The role of the case manager consists of four major functions: assessment, service planning, brokerage, and community intervention. This article sets forth the tasks and responsibilities of each function and, whenever possible, contrasts them with the present responsibilities of child welfare workers.

Assessment Case management begins with a service request or referral. The case manager then engages the clients in a process of diagnostic assessment.[6] Client assessment techniques in child welfare have been borrowed from psychology, sociology, child development, and learning theory. These models were not developed for child welfare practice and consequently have limited relevance to this purpose. The models either (1) exclude information needed to make case decisions, (2) consume inordinate amounts of time, or (3) require highly trained and educated persons to implement elaborate procedures. Some psychological models of assessment and diagnosis require certified testers. Social histories, long the basis for child welfare assessment, are not feasible in public agencies. With a few notable exceptions,

such as Phillips's work with the Child Welfare League of America, these
assessment approaches have not been integrated into a model that is
applicable to public child welfare.[7] Even the Phillips model has been
criticized as contributing to indecisiveness because it fails to focus attention on specific harms or to identify the minimum changes necessary to protect the child.[8] Direct service workers, lacking appropriate
assessment models and techniques, are forced to use unstructured,
idiosyncratic processes that do not insure that the necessary information is
collected and appropriate case plans developed.

Assessment tools need to be designed to guide workers in collecting
the information necessary to determine a permanent planning goal for
the child. Although it sounds appealing to improve a family's overall
functioning or to help them achieve their potential, realistically the
public agency's role is much narrower. In this era of increased reporting of child abuse and neglect, the state is called on to do something.
Unless care is exercised, the state will respond by intruding in family
situations, placing children inappropriately, and allowing children to
drift into long-term care.[9]

The first task in assessment is for the case manager to determine
whether the child has suffered or is likely to suffer serious harm and to
define those harms specifically. Harms include physical injury; sexual
abuse; serious emotional damage as evidenced by anxiety, depression,
withdrawal, or untoward aggression; or delinquency as a result of
parental encouragement, guidance, or approval. Furthermore, assessment should determine whether these harmful conditions exist as a
result of parental behavior or because of the parents' unwillingness to
seek corrective steps.[10]

The child welfare case manager must then determine which of the
four permanent planning goals is appropriate for the situation:
1. Maintain the child in his or her own home.
2. Return the child to his or her own home.
3. Move the child to adoption.
4. Move the child to independent living.
A fifth goal—protect the child from harm—is implicit in all child
welfare cases. The procedure of quickly establishing a broad planning
goal differs from most goal-setting systems used in current practice,
which tend to be open-ended and indefinite and to allow the goals to be
determined at the discretion of the caseworker through negotiation
with the client. Examples are problem-oriented recording (POR), task-
centered approaches, and the widely disseminated goal attainment
scaling. These devices may be appropriate for social service personnel

using therapy to change discrete behaviors, but the case manager must have a view of goals that reflects permanency planning.

Matching one of the four goals with the situation requires the exercise of professional discretion and experience with numerous comparable situations. This experience should be supported by a set of explicit criteria based on social work values and knowledge. For example, case managers often agonize over whether to maintain children in their own homes. Criteria based on "fulfilling the family's potential" or "the best interests of the children" are too vague to be of help. However, if case managers adopt the ideas of the nonintrusive state suggested by Wald and look for specific harms that a child is suffering or is likely to suffer, they will have criteria that are likely to protect the child and respect the autonomy of the family.[11] In the absence of specific harms and of a remedy that does more good than harm, the child is to be maintained in his or her own home. This approach makes it easy to develop criteria for each of the four goals.

The process of assessment is not unilateral. The worker involves the family and, when appropriate, the child in determining the goal and exploring each alternative. Although some workers are reluctant to discuss alternatives early in a case, there are indications that this is an important consideration. For example, the process of assessment is not the process of discovering and listing all the problems of the family. It is a process of negotiating a permanent planning goal with the client. All alternatives are discussed and the goal is selected according to specific, explicit criteria, which are matters of agency policy.

Service Planning   The service plan is the tangible, operational outcome of the assessment.[12] It begins with the negotiated goal, which is the product of assessment. The permanent planning goal becomes the shared goal of the agency and the client. Service planning, then, is determining with the client the services to be provided by the agency, the responsibilities of the clients, and how the service is to be provided; it also provides for periodic review.

For the case manager, the relevant question is not how to talk Mr. Jones into not drinking or into reducing the verbal battles he has with his 14-year-old son, Billy. The question is which service is most effective in reducing conflict between parent and child. For the case manager, case planning is service planning. This is an area in which social work research has let the case manager down. The manager needs to know, in some scientific sense, which services are effective for which situations, but social work research has provided little knowledge about the effectiveness of given services for the attainment of specific child welfare goals. Wiltse, after looking at the research, suggests comprehensive emergency services, day care, homemaker service, parent-child counseling, neighborhood-based environmental supports and diagnostic evaluation, and treatment as services that might prove effective in maintaining a child at home.[13] He concedes, however, that there is little evidence linking these services to the goal of maintaining a child at home, and he suggests that workers have "a list of resource alternatives to 'tick off' before concluding that placement must occur."[14] Although data on the effectiveness of services is scarce, Fischer has compiled a list of therapeutic techniques whose validity has been verified by extensive research.[15] Certainly there is no shortage of ideas for services for any of the child welfare goals. What is needed is an expanded emphasis on designing services for the attainment of each of the child welfare goals and experimentation on their effectiveness.

The knowledge now available suggests other elements that need to be included in the service plans. For example, if the goal is to return a child to the biological parents, research has indicated several critical factors, including the frequency of the parent's visits with the child and the frequency of the caseworker's contact with the natural parents.[16] The influence of these factors suggests that case managers should be required to plan for them, perhaps simply by including projected schedules for them as part of the service plan.

The involvement of the client in service planning and decision-making is consistent with social work values and democratic principles and is further supported by research indicating an increased success of services when this involvement occurs.[17] The service plan can be viewed as an agenda between the worker and the client. The client participates in the design of the plan and signs it. Although the primary client is the child, the parents are the ones most often involved in service planning, except when the goal is independent living or emancipation.

Brokering Services   The system of planning and purchasing services means that the public agency case manager acts as a broker between the client and the service provider. In assisting the client in purchasing a service, the case manager must be explicit about the subgoals to be accomplished by the service and the time it will take to achieve these goals.

Normally, a case manager has two sets of services from which to draw: the services contracted for by the public agency, and the services available from other agencies, such as mental health services, community action programs, or family service agencies. Case managers find it easier to specify goals and time frames and to receive monthly reports for services supplied by their own agency. However, even then it is tempting to be vague. Case managers must be prepared to specify, for example, homemaker instructions of four hours a week with the objective of teaching the client to prepare nutritious meals, rather than simply calling for four hours a week of homemaker services. Such definitions of services, moreover, should be related to specific harms the child faces.

Services available to a case manager but not purchased by the agency are more difficult to be specific about because case managers often feel that they cannot specify goals or time frames unless they are paying the bill. In mental health counseling, for example, it is not easy to question the presumed authority of the psychiatrist. Yet these services are usually publicly financed, and the social service professionals should be the most effective consumers of them. Contracts with explicit goals and time frames are just as appropriate for these services as they are for those purchased directly by the agency. An important element of service brokerage is the assistance the case manager provides the client in negotiating treatment contracts with appropriate service providers.

Community Intervention   All interactions with other institutions that impinge on the client fall under the category of community intervention. The institutions most frequently impinging on child welfare clients are the juvenile justice system, schools, and other public and voluntary social services in addition to employers, housing personnel, and recreation programs. Whereas most American families perform their own advocacy roles, children and parents involved with child welfare tend to be ineffective in their dealings with these institutions.

Acting as a mediator, a consultant, a program planner, and a public relations officer, the case manager performs a variety of functions designed to influence the decision-making of community persons. Advocacy in the juvenile justice system is probably the most complex form of community intervention. It includes collecting evidence, preparing court reports, and testifying in court on a wide variety of cases. The worker must have a knowledge of the structure, purpose, and functions of the juvenile justice system; of the rights of parents, children, and clients; and of confidentiality. This may seem self-evident, but a recent study in Illinois reported that workers' knowledge of relevant child welfare legislation, statutes, and standards was deficient.[18]

The schools are another important community agency. The child's right to an appropriate education is increasingly being recognized by society. The recent Education for All Handicapped Children Act is a good example of a mechanism to assure the extension of this right to a special population. Clients of the child welfare system are often the victims of a variety of social and institutional structures that can prevent the child from obtaining an adequate education. The case manager must know these structures, the rights of the child, and the sources of alternatives and possible recourse when a child is excluded from an appropriate education.

Naturally, there are a host of community agencies from which a case manager might obtain housing assistance, employment assistance, recreational opportunities, and so on. This type of advocacy might even be subcontracted as would any other service. However, case managers often neglect the type of community intervention by which they would exert leverage on behalf of a client. For example, if a state attorney will not pursue a case because he is too busy or does not think it is the kind of case to move on, he might be moved to reconsider by a phone call from a third party. Too often, child welfare agency staff have fallen into the mode of reacting to community pressure rather than actively exerting pressure on behalf of clients.

Supervision of Case Managers

Managing case loads does not involve sophisticated systems, models, or complex methodologies, yet case managers are generally unaware of many of the tasks they are to perform or are too involved in crisis intervention to maintain the perspective necessary to function effectively. Without proper direction and support, workers are likely to make inappropriate decisions, place children unnecessarily, and allow children to drift into long-term care. The key to this direction and support is the supervision process.

Supervision has long been considered a primary method by which social work practitioners are trained, supported, and monitored to insure that their actions are consistent with organizational policy. Despite its importance, supervision has been the subject of few empirical and systematic studies.[19] Most of the research involves case studies or theoretical discussions by educators.[20] The majority of the sophisticated studies in this area have been done in treatment settings and have focused on the satisfaction of supervisees with different supervisory styles. There is, therefore, little knowledge to help determine what makes supervision effective.

A study of supervisors that used the Leadership Opinion Questionnaire (LOQ) provides some guidance.[21] Not surprisingly, social work
supervisors tend to rate highly in terms of support, but have serious
deficiencies in regard to providing structure. If the case manager role
is to improve service outcomes, the supervisor must build a structure.

Often when supervisors go beyond the supportive function, they rely
on "keeping up with," or keeping informed of, their workers' caseloads
as the supervision strategy. Of course, supervisors do not attempt to
know the cases in the same detail as the workers; they rely on having a
sense of the cases. This concept is inadequate for several reasons. First,
this approach may mean that the supervisor must have knowledge of
four or five hundred cases. Second, the goal of keeping up with or
having a sense of a caseload is so nebulous that it fails to delineate
which elements or conditions of a case the supervisor should have a
knowledge of. In addition, this approach leads to open-ended discussions, often of considerable length, between workers and supervisors. One-on-one, most workers can talk around most cases, justifying
or rationalizing their decisions.

There are at least two measures the case management supervisor can
take to supply the needed structure. First, it is essential to set monthly
goals for the entire unit. The goal should be tied to the child welfare
goals previously mentioned. Examples of appropriate goals are maintaining a given number or percentage of children in their own homes,
moving a given number of children from foster care to their own
homes, and increasing by a certain amount the number of children
moving to adoption. Keeping the number of goals limited and tying
them to the child welfare goals set by the supervisor and the case
managers encourage the case managers to work their caseloads to find
the children who can return home or move to adoption. Goals of this
type provide a focus for both the workers and supervisors that does not
concentrate on blaming the worker, the family, or the child. They also
provide a focus for the case manager that goes beyond the resolution of
the current crises.

A second way supervisors can provide structure for effective case
management is case review. "Case review" is a term associated with a
variety of interpretations depending on the audience and the context.
The current uses of the term include the negative questioning of a
caseworker's decision; peer review, such as that by professional standards review organizations; informal supervisory review; and court
review.[22] In a study of worker decision-making, Luse found that workers were uncomfortable predicting case outcomes and setting comple-

tion dates. This led him to conclude that worker decision-making must be structured and a range of appropriate alternatives established.[23] Review systems need to be viewed as part of a system of administrative feedback. They need to be designed with a goal orientation, to include service planning, and to provide for periodic review. The review process should not take large amounts of time.

Essentially, an efficient case review system is one that is viewed as an agenda between the case managers and their supervisor. The agenda structures the interaction between the worker and the supervisor. It also provides the feedback which assures that cases are pursued, that criteria for goal setting or case closing are used, and that children are served in appropriate settings.

For the supervisor, the agenda is largely a set of goal-oriented questions. The following questions are examples:

- What is there about the situation that leads you to select this goal?
- What is there about this situation that leads you to select these services to obtain this goal?
- What would need to be done to obtain the goal sooner than you indicated?
- When do you think we will be able to close this case?

If the agenda is clear, the time spent on case review will be reduced, and workers will begin to anticipate the questions and plan cases accordingly. The addition of this structure to the supportive function that most social work supervisors perform well should keep the case manager focused on meeting child welfare goals as well as on resolving crises in the caseload.

Implementation

The article has sought to describe a revised job description for public child welfare workers. Many of the suggestions may seem obvious and elementary. Many of the ideas are not new; nor are they the original creations of the authors. However, the simplicity or obviousness is deceptive. The research overwhelmingly indicates that the suggestions are not simple and that the procedures they define are not generally followed. For example, one reason for the lack of permanent planning has been that many points of decision in the life of a case are delayed or ignored.[24] This situation highlights the most neglected aspect of policymaking, program design, and management in child welfare—implementation.

Although a prerequisite for success, an effective technology or a good idea is not a sufficient condition for implementation to occur. Studies conducted in public administration, management science, sociology, education, and community psychology have demonstrated that the dissemination of proved social innovations occurs slowly if at all.[25] Research on implementation has established two conditions for success: top level administrative support and the involvement of the users of the system, procedure, or strategy. Developing the case manager role requires administrators to set goals, delegate responsibilities, and define time frames. Supervisors and case managers must be involved in such tasks as designing contracting and assessment tools, defining specific criteria for state intervention and placement, and establishing procedures for regular case review. The failure of administrators to provide for lower level involvement increases the risk of sabotage and noncompliance and could undermine the development of case management.

Effective implementation could be enhanced by the activities of the federal government. First, funds should be appropriated for subsidized adoption. Currently, funds are available through Title XX for family support services and through Title IVA for foster care. Second, a research program with a focus on service effectiveness should be established. Services should include homemakers, day care, advocacy, and various forms of counseling. Case managers need to know which services are most effective at reaching what goals for which type of clients. Experimental and longitudinal designs offer the most promise.

Notes and References

1. Eugene Shinn, "Is Placement Necessary?" Unpublished Ph.D. thesis, Columbia University School of Social Work, 1968.

2. Dean Luse, *Child Placement Decisions* (Urbana, Ill.: School of Social Work, University of Illinois, 1975).

3. Arthur Emlen, *Is This Child Likely to Return Home?* (Portland, Oreg.: Regional Institute for Human Resources, July 1975).

4. Aaron Rosenblatt, "The Practitioners Use and Evaluation of Research," *Social Work*, 13 (January 1968), pp. 53–59.

5. Bill Benton et al., *Social Services: Federal Legislation vs. State Implementation* (Washington, D.C.: Urban Institute, October 1978), p. 117.

6. Robert O. Washington, *Case Management Manual for the Lorain Multi-Service Center* (Milwaukee, Wis.: School of Social Welfare, University of Wisconsin, 1975), p. 20.

7. Michael Phillips et al., *A Model for Intake Decisions in Child Welfare* (New York: Child Welfare League of America, 1972).

8. Kermit Wiltse, "Current Issues and New Directions in Foster Care," in *Child Welfare Strategy in the Coming Years*, Publication No. 78–30158 (Washington, D.C.: Department of Health, Education & Welfare, 1978), pp. 51–89.

9. Michael S. Wald, "State Intervention on Behalf of Neglected Children: Standards for Removal of Chidren from Their Homes, Monitoring the Status of Children in Foster Care, and Termination of Parental Rights," *Stanford Law Review*, 28 (April 1976), pp. 623–706.

10. Ibid., p. 701.

11. Ibid.

12. Washington, op. cit., p. 33.

13. Wiltse, op. cit., pp. 67–72.

14. Wiltse, op. cit., p. 68.

15. Joel Fischer, *Effective Casework Practice: An Eclectic Approach* (New York: McGraw-Hill Book Co., 1978).

16. Charles A. Rapp and John Poertner, "Reducing Foster Care: Critical Factors and Administrative Strategies," *Administration in Social Work*, 2 (Fall 1978), pp. 335–346.

17. Theodore J. Stein, Eileen D. Gambrill, and Kermit Wiltse, "Foster Care: The Use of Contracts," *Public Welfare*, 32 (Fall 1974), pp. 20–25.

18. Charles Henderson and Barbara Meddin, "Evaluation of the Title XX Child Advocacy Training Grant: Legal Aspects Pretest" (Urbana, Ill.: School of Social Work, University of Illinois, 1980). (Mimeographed.)

19. Alfred Kadushin, *Supervision in Social Work* (New York: Columbia University Press, 1976); Scott Briar, "Family Services and Casework," in Henry S. Maas, ed., *Research in the Social Services: A Five-Year Review* (New York: National Association of Social Workers, 1971), p. 111; and Briar, "Family Services," in Maas, ed., *Five Fields of Service* (New York: National Association of Social Workers, 1966), p. 49.

20. Carlton Munson, ed., *Social Work Supervision: Classic Statements and Critical Issues* (New York: The Free Press, 1979), p. 240.

21. Donald K. Granvold, "Training Social Work Supervisors to Meet Organizational and Worker Objectives," *Journal of Education for Social Work*, 14 (Spring, 1978), pp. 38–45.

22. John Poertner and Charles A. Rapp, "Information System Design in Foster Care," *Social Work*, 25 (March 1980), pp. 114–119.

23. Luse, op. cit.

24. Emlen, op. cit.

25. Matthew Miles, "Some Properties of Schools as Social Systems," in Goodwin Watson, ed., *Change in School Systems* (Union, N.J.: Cooperative Project for Educational Development, 1967), pp. 1–29; and George Fairweather, Daniel H. Sanders, and Louis G. Tornatzky, *Creating Change in Mental Health Organizations* (New York: Pergamon Press, 1974).

7

Social Work Research: What's the Use?

Charles D. Cowger and Jill Doner Kagle

Forging a strong link between research and practice is a crucial task for the social work profession in the 1980s. If social work is to respond meaningfully to the needs of clients, the demands of funding sources, and the encroachment of other professions, it must both support research on practice and use research in practice.

This study focuses on the utility of research knowledge in practice. It explores the question of whether the empirical research published in social work journals is useful to the practitioner.

In the 1970s, social work's goal of improving its knowledge base gave impetus to increased research activity. More of the articles in social work journals presented empirical studies; two journals that concentrated principally on social service research began publication. As the amount of research produced increased, attention was focused on the utilization of research by practitioners.

The social work practitioner (here broadly defined as someone employed in the organization and delivery of social work services) has been the subject of several studies on research utilization. Casselman showed that practitioners did not find research helpful in formulating treatment plans or improving practice.[1] Two studies found that, in workers' opinions, articles on research findings, including those on practice methods, ranked far below supervision and consultation in improving their practice.[2] In another study, Weed and Greenwald found that workers read few research reports and that they were unable to identify correctly some commonly used statistical symbols.[3]

Although these studies provide important descriptive evidence that these workers were not using research knowledge to inform practice, the samples do not permit generalization to all social work practitioners. One study, however, used a random sample of the members of the National Association of Social Workers (NASW) and thus permits generalization.[4] Workers were asked to evaluate a research study. They were able to distinguish between "good" (control group) and "bad" (no control group) designs, but were more influenced by the findings of the study, namely, whether casework treatment was found to be effective. The study also found that the majority of workers do not participate in research and that they do not consult research in "difficult practice situations."

The subject of all these research studies was the social work practitioner—the worker's attitudes, knowledge, and activities. The solutions the articles offered to the problem of research utilization also focused on the worker. If research is to have an impact on social work practice, it must be understood, valued, and used by practitioners. Certainly this is an important goal. However, changing practitioners' knowledge of and attitude toward research may not, by itself, increase the utilization of research findings in practice unless the research carried out and published is relevant to the issues confronted by practitioners. Presented with many of the empirical studies currently published, the practitioner may validly ask, "What's the use?"

Determining Practice Utility

In contrast with earlier studies on research utilization that focused on the practitioner, this study focuses on social work research itself. Research articles published in social work journals were analyzed for their practice utility.

The first problem to resolve in this project was to establish rules for determining the potential utility of research for the practitioner. The three criteria used to judge potential utility were (1) the guidelines provided for practice must be explicit, (2) practice guidelines must be logically derived from the findings, and (3) the nature of the practice studied must be specified.

Is all research related to social work, its clients, and its environment ultimately usable? Perhaps, but this argument is self-defeating: if everything is equally valued, the problem of discrimination again belongs to the practitioner. Must research focus on individual practice behavior to be useful? Probably not. This would be too narrow a definition of social work practice. To avoid criteria that are either too narrow or too general and to assess the explicitness of guidelines for practice, the following rules were followed: a study must either test a practice proposition, or a practice proposition or directive must be derived from its findings. Reid has suggested that theory-building for practice be based on propositions that take the form, "In situation x, intervention y is likely to result in outcome z."[5] The present study categorized this form of statement about practice as a "practice proposition" and was less stringent than Reid in its definition of practice propositions; it did not require that situation x be defined. Propositions such as "intervention y is likely to result in outcome z" were accepted as practice propositions. In this study "practice directive," like "practice proposition," was defined as a generalization that provides a practice guideline or principle. However, unlike the practice proposition, practice directives typically do not specify consequences. Practice directives that are based on research findings are often stated in the form, "Based on the data, one ought to do. . . ." Although practice directives may also be based on values or theoretical orientations, those based on research findings were the concern of the study.

Another criterion of practice utility was that the logic of any practice propositions or practice directives derived from the findings must be apparent. When practice propositions or practice directives presented in a research report have no clear linkage to the study's findings, the report misleads the practitioner because the proposition or directive is neither supported nor rejected on the basis of the research data. Although such practice propositions or directives may be interesting to the practitioner, they are not research based. Therefore, studies without clear links between their practice propositions or directives and the research findings were classified as research without practice utility.

Specific definition of the nature of the practice studied in the research is a necessary condition for practice utilization. Without a clear statement of, for example, what a worker did or how a program was run, practitioners reading the research report are not able to duplicate the practice in their own work. The need to be specific in the definition of practice has been a recurrent theme in recent social work literature.[6] A study was judged to have practice utility only if the nature of practice was sufficiently specified that it could be duplicated in practice or replicated in research.

Method and Sample

To assess the utility of published social work research, the authors reviewed research published in *Social Work, Social Service Review, Social Casework,* and *Child Welfare* between 1974 and 1978. These journals were selected because of their historic tradition in the field and for the size of their readership. All articles that reported quantitative analysis of data, such as the use of percentages, measures of central tendencies, or tests of significance, were included in the study. This resulted in the selection of 270 articles.

The instrument used to determine research utility made the following differentiations: Does the research test practice propositions, derive practice propositions, or provide direction for practice? Is the dependent variable specified, making replication possible? Are the practice propositions or directives put forward in the report tied logically to the findings? Additional information was gathered on each article including the occupation of the authors, the field and type of practice that was the subject of the research, the type and source of statistics used, whether a control or comparison group was used, the type of instrument used, and whether the research was a program evaluation. The instrument was tested, reworked, and tested again. Three readers worked on the project, and each article was read and coded by two readers. When there was a disagreement in coding, a third reader read the article, made an independent judgment, and negotiated a consensus.

Table 1 shows the number of articles included in the study by journal and year. There was an increase in the number of research articles published from 1974 to 1975; since then, the number published has remained remarkably steady, except for a slight increase in 1977. Fifty-three percent (144) of the articles were written by authors with academic affiliations, 24 percent (66) were written by practitioners, and 17 percent (47) were written jointly by academics and practitioners. One or more of the authors were identified as social workers in 68 percent (183) of the articles. Only 24 percent (66) were authored by non–social workers.

The research reported in these articles dealt with a variety of social problems, practice issues, program arrangements, and client groups from virtually every field in which social workers practice. Social work practice, however, was the subject of only 60 percent (162) of the articles. Direct practice (casework, group work, or family therapy) was the subject of 21 percent (56) of the studies, and indirect practice (community organization, administration, or policy analysis) was the

TABLE 1.
NUMBER OF RESEARCH ARTICLES BY JOURNAL AND YEAR

Journal	Year					Cumulative Number of Articles	Percentage
	1974	1975	1976	1977	1978		
Social Work	17	20	23	29	22	111	41.2
Social Service Review	8	18	13	12	13	64	23.7
Social Casework	5	8	4	7	5	29	10.7
Child Welfare	14	9	15	13	15	66	24.4
Total	44	55	55	61	55	270	100.0

subject of 33 percent (89) of the studies. The practice studied in the remaining 6 percent (18) of the articles was difficult to classify; it was sometimes generic, sometimes primarily educational, and sometimes not clearly described. Forty percent (107) of the articles were not practice focused. They reported, for example, demographic studies or professional attitudes. Of the 162 articles on practice, 72 were evaluation reports of individual programs.

Findings

Only 30 percent (81) of the studies had practice utility as defined in this study: they tested or derived practice propositions or directives, the independent variable was specified, and the conclusions were logically tied to the findings. (See Table 2.) Included in this category were 34 studies that tested practice propositions, 25 studies that derived practice propositions, and 22 studies that derived practice directives. Seventy percent (189) of the articles had no explicit application to practice. They were excluded from having utility for the following reasons. Seventeen percent (45) of the studies had practice propositions or directives, but the independent variable was not sufficiently defined to allow practice implementation or research replication. Thirty-four percent (93) of the studies provided no practice propositions or directives. Nineteen percent (51) of the studies presented propositions or directives not tied logically to the research findings.

The generalizability of the 81 studies judged to have practice utility was limited. Only 29 of them used control or comparison groups, and only 12 used random procedures for selection of a sample. Only 4 of the articles that were judged to be useful to practitioners used both control groups and random procedures. Thirteen percent (34) of the studies tested propositions in the manner proposed by Reid. However,

TABLE 2.

TABULATION OF RESEARCH ARTICLES FOR USEFULNESS TO PRACTICE

Criteria of Utility	Number of Articles	Percent (N = 270)
Studies providing practice guidelines		
Practice proposition tested, independent variable specified, proposition tied to findings	34	12.6
Practice proposition derived, independent variable specified, proposition tied to findings	25	9.3
Practice directive derived, independent variable specified, directive tied to findings	22	8.1
Total	81	30.0
Studies not providing practice guidelines		
Propositions or directives tied to findings, but independent variable not specified	45	16.7
No practice propositions or directives introduced	93	34.4
Propositions or directives introduced, but not tied to the research findings	51	18.9
Total	189	70.0

the ability to generalize from these studies was also limited in that only 24 studies that tested practice propositions used control or comparison groups and only 4 used random procedures for selecting the sample.

One might expect to find that articles by practitioners would be more likely to test or generate practice propositions or directives. However, as indicated in Table 3, this was not the case. Thirty-three percent (45) of the studies by academicians provided practice propositions or directives, and only 25 percent (16) of the studies by practitioners did so. The research combination of academician and practitioner had the best record with 40 percent (19) of their studies generating practice propositions or directives.

Discussion

The research published in the four social work journals reviewed for this study does not provide an ample resource for the discovery of new practice knowledge. No wonder that social workers do not value or use research in their practice; the research available to them through these social work journals offers them little with clear application to practice. A cursory review of other social work journals indicated that this finding is typical of social work literature in general. However, a similar study of new journals should be made to test this observation.

TABLE 3.
AUTHORSHIP OF PRACTICE-RELEVANT RESEARCH ARTICLES

Criteria of Utility	Number of Articles by Academicians[a]	Number of Articles by Practitioners and Academicians	Number of Articles by Practitioners[a]
Studies providing practice guidelines			
Practice proposition tested, independent variable specified, proposition tied to findings	21	9	4
Practice proposition derived, independent variable specified, proposition tied to findings	13	7	5
Practice directive derived, independent variable specified, directive tied to findings	11	3	7
Studies not providing practice guidelines			
Propositions or directives tied to findings, but independent variable not specified	22	6	13
No practice propositions or directives introduced	47	18	22
Propositions or directives introduced, but not tied to the research findings	30	4	14
Total[b]	144	47	65

[a] These categories include articles coauthored by students.
[b] These figures do not include nine studies written solely by students and five studies for which information on the authors was not available.

If research utilization is to be improved in the 1980s, the problems reflected in the findings of this study must be solved. Authors and editors should be sensitive to the following issues:

1. The obvious strategy to increase utility is to examine practice as the subject of the research. To do this, the independent variable—the subject of the research—must be practice behavior, a practice model, service arrangements, or service programs.

2. It is not necessary that methodologically flawed research be withheld. On the contrary, research that takes place in the real world

typically must sacrifice scientific rigor for validity. However, authors should note the methodological problems to assist the reader in assessing the generalizability of the findings.

3. Logical flaws often reflect the prejudgments of the researchers. It is always difficult to maintain neutrality in research situations. One possible solution is to use outsiders in the research effort. For example, academicians could work with practitioners in agency-based research; or practitioners could test out a model of practice proposed by an academician. Of course, such collaboration requires working through old conflicts, but it may be worth the effort.

4. Practice that is the subject of a research investigation needs to be described clearly. A practice idea cannot be used by others if the author does not specify what was done.

This study suggests that the profession needs to direct additional attention to promoting research utilization in social work practice. Research studies in social work journals, most of which were found to have little utility for practitioners, should be improved in form and content. Such improvement should be the responsibility not only of those conducting the research, but also of funding sources, of journal editors, and of the professional organization.

Notes and References

1. Betsy-Lea Casselman, "On the Practitioner's Orientation toward Research," *Smith College Studies in Social Work*, 42 (June 1972), pp. 211–233.

2. Casselman, op. cit.; and Aaron Rosenblatt, "The Practitioner's Use and Evaluation of Research," *Social Work*, 13 (January 1968), pp. 53–59.

3. Patricia Weed and Shayna R. Greenwald, "The Mystics of Statistics," *Social Work*, 18 (March 1973), pp. 113–115.

4. Stuart A. Kirk and Joel Fischer, "Do Social Workers Understand Research?" *Journal of Education for Social Work*, 12 (Winter 1976), pp. 63–70; and Stuart A. Kirk, Michael J. Osmalov, and Joel Fischer, "Social Workers' Involvement in Research," *Social Work* 21 (March 1976), pp. 121–124.

5. For a discussion of Reid's suggestion that if a practice theory is to be viable, it must contain a number of such propositions that have a "high probability of being confirmed when specifically applied," *see* William J. Reid, "Social Work for Social Problems," *Social Work*, 22 (September 1977), p. 379.

6. *See* Joel Fischer, "Is Casework Effective?" *Social Work*, 18 (January 1973), pp. 5–20; Walter W. Hudson, "First Axioms of Treatment," *Social Work*, 23 (January 1978), pp. 65–66; and Aaron Rosen and Enola Proctor, "Specifying the Treatment Process: The Basis for Effective Research," *Journal of Social Service Research*, 2 (Winter 1978), p. 33.

8

Legal and Ethical Issues of Informed Consent

JoAnn Betts,
Karen Authier,
Susan Salladay, and
James D. Sherrets

The dilemmas posed by the issue of informed consent—the duty of a clinician or researcher to inform a client or subject of the possible risks and benefits of a treatment or experiment—demand that social workers and other helping professionals develop innovative approaches to balancing the interests of the client against the need to expand professional knowledge through experimentation on human subjects. This article discusses the ethical and legal issues related to informed consent and explores their implications for the practitioner or investigator.

In the 1970s, Americans witnessed a significant shifting of attitudes toward the helping professions. The previous, almost godlike authority of the practitioner came to be challenged frequently in the office or hospital, in the press, and in the courts. The public sector became increasingly aware of clients' rights and of the impact controversial research could have on community values. With this awareness came a belief that professional skill does not insure moral competence.

Many factors contributed to this process of growing disillusionment, or what Starr called the "waning of professional sovereignty."[1] The public became outraged over the skyrocketing costs of health care, especially in the light of the uneven allocation and accessibility of services. Consumerism grew and with it the demand for egalitarian, contract-based client-practitioner relationships. A strong clients' rights movement developed around the belief that the rights of the individual supersede the rights or needs of society. Professional advocates of clients' rights and carefully constructed peer review boards began to monitor treatment and research. The rise of alternative, lay-based human service systems, such as Parents Anonymous, Recovery Incorporated, and self-help health clinics, also contributed to the dissatisfaction with professional caregivers.

A clear understanding of the prevailing mood concerning health care, human services, and human investigation is necessary to a consideration of informed consent because it was from this milieu that the present problems and ambiguities surrounding informed consent emerged. The issue touches clients or patients who must rely on the integrity of the professional for the information they need to make informed decisions. Patients rely on professionals to decide what information is relevant and how best to present it; they also rely on lawyers, educators, and ethicists who are concerned with the formation of public policy, professional standards, and moral guidelines.

Question of Ethics and Law

Why is the issue of informed consent one that concerns ethics? Ethics, which may be broadly defined as the systematic study of all moral beliefs, principles, and practices, attempts to observe and define the human behavior that results from values, priorities, commitments, and judgments about right and wrong. The notion of informed consent involves practitioners, researchers, and clients in making judgments about what is right, best, or good, especially when risks must be weighed against benefits or when one human right or value conflicts with another right or value.

Current attitudes and the history of exploitation of research subjects make the issue of informed consent a volatile one. There exists no general agreement about what is or ought to constitute informed consent or whether the responsibility for becoming informed rests with the investigator, the subject, or a neutral third party. Further, no standard has been established for accomplishing truly informed consent. At present, the procedures are left to the discretion and integrity of the researcher.

Particularly difficult ethical issues regarding informed consent emerge when research protocols call for subjects who constitute especially vulnerable client populations, such as children, mentally retarded individuals, and those whose judgment and will may be impaired by mental illness. Yet it is precisely these people for whom research is needed, and breakthroughs could be dramatically beneficial.

Other difficult issues of informed consent include the matter of the fine line dividing research from treatment; the problem of patients in large institutions who find themselves involved in multiple projects, yet with each researcher working independently; the issues surrounding the use of full or limited guardianships for totally or partially incompetent subjects to enhance normalization and also to prevent exploitation; and the question of institutional jeopardy that arises when professionals who wear two hats, researcher and provider of treatment, subtly pressure institutionalized patients to participate in an experiment.

Over the last several decades, ethical principles of informed consent have become canonized in case and administrative law: the unauthorized touching of a person came to constitute the common law tort of battery; a person who assumed a position of trust and confidence in a fiduciary relationship became liable for any misrepresentations, whether by affirmative statement or by nondisclosure; and the rights of patients to self-determination were established, including the right to refuse treatment. It must be understood that the theory of informed consent, like most legal doctrine, has not developed through a linear progression of landmark court decisions with applications in all jurisdictions, but rather through a complex maze of often conflicting and inconsistent court decisions that came from many different jurisdictions.

With regard to liability, it is important for the clinician-investigator to know that patients have sued successfully when procedures were performed without their informed consent, regardless of the need for the procedure or the skill with which it was performed. Plaintiffs in various suits have used either of two basic legal theories to support their actions. First, a procedure performed without the patient's knowledge or authorization has been identified as the tort of assault and battery.[2] Second, the physician's failure to explain the consequences of a procedure to which a patient has consented has been categorized as negligence.[3]

There are differences in the two causes of action. If assault and battery is alleged, no expert testimony is required to prove it; if negligence is alleged, expert witnesses must testify that the clinician or investigator violated certain standards for disclosure. There has been much debate over how much detail a clinician or investigator must disclose. In *Natanson* v. *Kline,* the case usually cited as initiating the doctrine of informed consent, the court decided that the standard of practice in the community should be the basis for determining how much patients should be told.[4] Then, in the early 1970s, two appellate decisions, *Canterbury* v. *Spence* in Washington, D.C., and *Cobbs* v. *Grant* in California, rejected the medical model of standard of practice in favor of the new rule of the reasonable, prudent patient as the standard by which juries decide whether a patient would have withheld consent to the procedure had all material risk been disclosed.[5] A second difference in the two causes of action is that the statute of limitations may be longer in some states for a negligence action than for a battery action. Third, since a battery is considered an intentional tort, punitive damages are available in most states; such damages would not apply in negligence actions. Of greatest concern to the professional is the exception in most malpractice insurance coverage for intentional torts or batteries.

Although much of the case law establishing principles of informed consent has involved issues of medical treatment, case law will probably build on the growing body of administrative law regarding research issues. The most stunning example in recent history of the lack of informed consent to research participation involved the atrocities of medical experimentation in Nazi Germany. Out of the subsequent Nuremburg court decision came the currently accepted principles regarding the extent of disclosure and the three elements of informed consent:

> The voluntary consent of the human subject is absolutely essential. This means that the person involved should have legal capacity to give consent; should be so situated as to be able to exercise free power of choice . . .; and should have sufficient knowledge and comprehension of the elements of the subject matter involved as to enable him to make an understanding and enlightened decision. . . . There should be made known to him the nature, duration, and purpose of the experiment; the method and means by which it is to be conducted; all inconveniences and hazards reasonable to be expected; and the effects upon his health or person which may possibly come from his participation in the experiment.[6]

These principles have been reiterated by the National Commission for the Protection of Human Subjects of Biomedical and Behavioral Research, which was established in 1974 by Congress to protect vulnerable populations from exploitation as research subjects. In November 1978, the Department of Health, Education and Welfare (DHEW)

published a set of proposed rules regarding research with institutionalized, mentally disabled individuals that were based on the
commission's guidelines.[7] Although a complete analysis of the DHEW
rules is beyond the scope of this article, it is noted that the regulations
reflect a legal trend toward (1) more stringent or mandatory reviews of
proposed research protocols and informed consent procedures—for
example, the commission provided institutional review boards with the
authority to appoint consent auditors—and (2) mandatory court or
quasi-judicial approval of participation in research by incompetent
subjects. DHEW invited public comment on a proposed amendment
that would require that subjects be advised as to the availability of
financial compensation for and medical treatment of injuries incurred
from research. Thus, it appears that there will soon be both administrative and case law precedents for the liability of the investigator for
injuries incurred by research subjects.

Implications for Practice and Research

Social workers may be confronted with dilemmas posed by informed
consent in two capacities, as researchers who must obtain informed
consent from vulnerable clients and as direct service workers who have
responsibilities as advocates for their clients. To further confuse the
issue, the practitioner, as mentioned earlier, may be wearing two hats in
dealing with the same individual, one of researcher and the other of
service provider or clinician. In such situations it is important that the
practitioner acknowledge the areas of ethical conflict, which include the
researcher's vested interest in obtaining subjects. The historical emphasis in social work education on the development of self-awareness as a
crucial prerequisite to work with clients can be expected to make social
workers particularly well-equipped to recognize such conflicts of interest. However, with increasing pressure on social workers, especially
those affiliated with academic institutions, to produce research as a
prerequisite to professional recognition and advancement, social work
investigators must be increasingly on guard lest the pressures lead to a
sacrifice of responsible ethical standards and the adoption of what
Luria described as "the ethics of competitive enterprise."[8]

Sensitivity to the conflict of interest and the vulnerability of certain
populations does not preclude research efforts by social workers. It
should, however, motivate social workers to develop creative methods
and procedures that are in keeping with the evolving criteria for informed consent. The development of new approaches to obtaining

informed consent must adapt the general ethical and legal requirements described earlier to specific populations and specific research activities.

Definition of Informed Consent Although disagreement abounds, the doctrine of informed consent may be broadly defined as the duty of a clinician or investigator to warn a patient or research subject of the anticipated benefits, expected results, and possible risks of a proposed treatment or experimental condition. If a patient or subject does not understand this information, any consent he or she gives will probably be called an uninformed assent and be held legally invalid.

Despite the lack of consensus regarding an exact definition of the term, some basic parameters must be considered in obtaining informed consent. If prospective research subjects are suspected of being incompetent, the researcher must carefully evaluate the three elements of informed consent: (1) capacity, (2) voluntariness, and (3) information. All three elements should be addressed by the procedures used to obtain consent. The first element, the capacity of the subject to give informed consent, is a variable that the researcher must assess and recognize, but that the researcher cannot control. The other two elements, information and voluntariness, are controlled by the researcher.[9] However, the three elements are interdependent. For instance, capacity affects the individual's ability to understand and evaluate the information provided by the researcher; the capacity of the prospective subject and the quality and quantity of information provided affect the individual's interpretation of the voluntariness of the consent. Therefore, proposed improvements in the process of obtaining informed consent may focus on one of the elements of consent, but must take cognizance of the interactive aspects of the three elements.

Capacity of the Subject "Capacity" is defined as "the present ability to acquire or retain knowledge; the ability to do something; a faculty or aptitude; the legal qualification or authority to perform an act."[10] Any definition of capacity must take into account the three parameters of capacity: (1) a person's age, (2) a person's competence, and (3) a particular situation, including the complexity of the information to be understood. Of particular interest to human service researchers is the current emphasis on the principle of situational capacity—the ability to give informed consent in certain straightforward, no-risk situations, but not in highly complex, potentially risky situations. A clinical evaluation of a subject's adaptive behavior and life experiences must supplement measures of innate intelligence in determining the situations in which a person may be able to give legally relevant and effective consent.

Many researchers use the legal standard of de jure incompetence for determining which patients are capable of giving informed consent. This is a dangerous standard for ethical and legal practice because even though patients have not been adjudicated legally incompetent (de jure incompetence), this does not mean they are not incompetent in fact (de facto incompetence). Most professionals are aware of the large numbers of mentally handicapped individuals who have not been brought before a judge for a competency hearing, but whose judgment is so impaired that they are unable to handle their daily affairs, much less make informed decisions regarding participation in complex, technical research projects.

Assessment of the capacity of subjects has become more imperative in view of the trends toward the deinstitutionalization of mentally impaired individuals and the decrease in legal designations of incompetence with the resulting appointments of guardians. Although the decrease in guardianships has many positive advantages in helping the handicapped individual with the process of normalization, these are disadvantages and risks in that the individual is vulnerable to exploitation in many areas of life, including research. Also, although many institutions failed to take adequate measures to protect residents from unethical researchers, the ethical researcher at least was provided with foreknowledge of the subject's handicapping condition by virtue of the subject's institutional status. It has now become the responsibility of the researcher to assess each subject and arrive at a decision regarding that subject's competency to provide consent. To satisfy the criteria of informed consent, the subject must be able to comprehend the possible benefits of participation in the study, the potential risks of participation, the degree to which the research would be physically or psychologically intrusive, the degree of irreversibility of the research and research procedures, and the alternatives to participation. These tasks of comprehension might perplex a college graduate; yet social workers routinely expect individuals who have a variety of mental and intellectual handicaps to make such decisions. Can a depressed individual realistically look out for his or her own best interests? Does a senile nursing home resident have the capacity to understand the degree of intrusiveness or the alternatives to participation in research? Does a moderately retarded individual understand the potential risks or benefits?

The researcher may determine that a prospective subject who has not been declared legally incompetent nevertheless lacks the capacity for informed consent. For such situations, it is imperative that options be developed which protect the prospective subject without unduly limiting self-determination, the right of an individual to make choices regarding his or her own life. One possibility is the development of collateral or substitute agents to assist the individual with consent decisions. For instance, in some states the concept of limited guardianship has been recognized by statute.[11] Under limited guardianship, individuals are judged to be partially competent and are not deprived of legal self-determination in all areas of life, but only in those areas where they lack skill or ability. Limited guardianships, therefore, are one vehicle for protecting the mentally handicapped from exploitation in research activities. However, Horner emphasizes that the use of limited guardianship depends not only on the revision of state laws, but also on paring the costs of obtaining guardians, or alleviating the emotional burden of guardianship for the guardian, and on attending to the potential for conflict of interest situations in which the guardians may be tempted to make decisions in their own, rather than the handicapped individual's best interest.[12]

Other ways of protecting subjects whose competency is questionable are to use court or quasi-judicial reviews without appointment of a guardian and to increase the use of patient advocates.[13] Patient advocates might be trained volunteers who have no vested interest in the research project or in the institution in which the research is conducted. Patient advocates would be expected to act in the patient's best interest by raising questions and making inquiries into areas of concern for the patient. The use of a patient advocate has the advantage of providing a patient with an ally without imposing the stigma of guardianship or the awesome and possibly frightening experience of a formal court proceeding.

Voluntariness The second element of informed consent, voluntariness, is the extent to which a prospective subject is "able to exercise free power of choice without the intervention of any element of force, fraud, deceit, duress, overreaching or other ulterior form of constraint or coercion."[14] A subject's voluntariness is colored by the environment and the relationships involved. Obviously, patients who live in institutions or who are being asked for their consent by their primary therapist or physician who has control over their hospital discharge, civil commitment status, eligibility for financial aid, referral to commu-

nity agencies, and so on are under more overt or covert coercion than
subjects who do not reside in institutions or who are giving consent to
neutral researchers who are not perceived as having power over their
lives. In the *New England Journal of Medicine,* Ingelfinger states his
belief that hospitalized patients are not adequately protected by informed consent doctrines because of this very element of covert coercion:

> Incapacitated and hospitalized because of illness, frightened by strange and
> impersonal routines, and fearful for his/her health and perhaps life, he/she
> is far from exercising a free power of choice when the person to whom
> he/she anchors all his/her hopes asks, "Say, you wouldn't mind, would you,
> if you joined some of the other patients on this floor and helped us to carry
> out some very important research we are doing."[15]

Voluntariness mandates the researcher to ensure not only that the
patient has the option of refusing to participate in the research, but
also that the individual has a clear understanding of that option. Pellegrino emphasizes the importance of recognizing the subtle and covert
forms of coercion, such as the subject's desire to please, the mystique
surrounding research, and uncritical veneration of the scientist, as well
as the more overt forms of coercion.[16] Patient advocates can be used to
minimize coercive factors, and independent review mechanisms with
investigating and enforcement powers are essential when there is some
expectation that the prospective subject has reason to perceive intimi-
dation or coercion in the request for consent.

Information Provided   With respect to the third element necessary
for informed consent, the provision of information, the researcher
must pay attention to the substance of the information for which
consent is being sought and to the manner in which the information is
communicated. It is not sufficient for the researchers to deliver the
information; they are compelled to design the communication of the
information in such a way that it is understood by the individual
subject, with all his or her unique handicaps. There is a real need for
the development of creative procedures for providing information to
prospective subjects that take into account the subject's mental limitations. Standard procedures for obtaining informed consent entail
providing information to the individual in written form along with
verbal interpretation of the information. Since individuals with mental
handicaps or other limitations may have difficulty comprehending the
information if the format is oriented to a nonhandicapped population,
the researcher must analyze the methods of presenting the information

with respect to the unique capabilities and limitations of the prospective subject. For instance, the use of simplified language, programmed learning, or audiovisual aids may enhance the possibility for comprehension.

Another approach to assessing the prospective subject's comprehension of material is to use two-part forms, the first part containing the necessary information and the second part constituting a questionnaire that measures the individual's comprehension of the material presented in the first section. Miller and Willner suggest that the questionnaire section include approximately five questions covering the basic categories of information: benefits, risks, inconveniences, purposes, alternatives to participation, and tasks.[17] There is also value in using delayed tests to measure comprehension. Delayed tests are especially important in dealing with subjects who have difficulties with memory or recall. Like presentations of information, tests for comprehension must be developed in oral or primary language formats for individuals who have difficulty reading or for whom English is a second language.

Clinical-research meetings involving subjects, researchers, and clinicians provide another means for providing opportunities for questions, answers, and discussions.[18] There are many advantages to use of a group approach. Subjects are often more comfortable raising questions and expressing fears or concerns in a setting that includes peers than in one-to-one sessions with professionals. However, if the meetings are conducted on a regular basis, it should be recognized that a group process would evolve which could either support or interfere with the research goals and design.

In addition to measures that can be taken by researchers, other persons who have less direct involvement with research can help in the effort to protect the rights of research subjects. For instance, editors of journals publishing research literature can refuse to publish work that does not meet established ethical criteria.[19]

There is an increasing recognition of the importance of incorporating the study of ethical issues into professional education programs.[20] In the final analysis, the best protection for a research subject is an investigator who has been taught to consider questions of ethics as issues of primary importance. As Pellegrino eloquently states, "No set of legal or institutional constraints can guard against the cumulative evil that subtly evolves from small indifferences."[21]

In summary, these and many other issues related to informed consent need clear and unbiased investigation. Social workers and other helping professionals must inquire fully and sensitively into various methods of presenting informed consent requests to vulnerable research subjects and develop methods that maximize such subjects' comprehension and assure their human rights.

Notes and References

1. Paul Starr, "Medicine and the Waning of Professional Sovereignty," *Daedalus*, 107 (Winter 1978), pp. 175–192.

2. *See*, for example, Pratt v. Davis, 118 Ill. App. 161 (1905); affirmed on rehearing, 224 Ill. App. 300, 79 N.E. 562 (1906); Mohr v. Williams, 95 Minn. 261, 104 N.W. 12 (1905); and Schloendorff v. Society of New York Hospitals, 211 N.Y.S. 125, 104 N.E. 92 (1914).

3. *See*, for example, Salgo v. Leland Stanford, Jr., University Board of Trustees, 154 Cal. App. 2d 560, 317 P 2d 170 (1957); and Joy v. Y.S. Chau, 377 N.E. 2d 670, (Ind., 1978).

4. Natanson v. Kline, 186 Kans. 393, 350 P 2d 1093 (1960).

5. Canterbury v. Spence, 464 F 2d 772 (D.C. Cir. 1972); and Cobbs v. Grant, 104 Cal Rptr 505, 8 Cal. 3d 229, 502 P 2d 1 (1972).

6. Nuremburg Trials (1945), cited by Jay Katz, *Experimentation with Human Beings*, (New York: Russell Sage Foundation, 1972), pp. 302–304.

7. Department of Health, Education and Welfare, *Federal Register*, 43, November 17, 1978, pp. 53950–53956; and the National Commission for the Protection of Human Subjects of Biomedical and Behavioral Research, *Report and Recommendations: Research Involving Those Institutionalized as Mentally Infirm; Report and Recommendations: Research Involving Children; Report and Recommendations: Institutional Review Boards* (Washington, D.C.: U.S. Government Printing Office, 1975–1978).

8. Salvador E. Luria, "On Research Styles and Allied Matters," *Daedalus*, 98 (Summer 1969), pp. 480–501.

9. Robert H. Horner, "Accountability in Habilitation of the Severely Retarded: The Issue of Informed Consent," *American Association for the Education of the Severely and Profoundly Handicapped*, 4 (March 1979), pp. 24–35.

10. H. Rutherford Turnbull III, ed., *Consent Handbook* (Washington, D.C.: American Association on Mental Deficiency, 1977), p. 6.

11. Horner, op. cit., p. 30.

12. Ibid.

13. J. Annas George, *The Rights of Hospital Patients: The Basic ACLU Guide to a Hospital Patient's Rights* (New York: Avon Books, 1975), Chap. 18.

14. Turnbull, op. cit., p. 10.

15. Franz J. Ingelfinger, "Informed (But Uneducated) Consent," *New England Journal of Medicine,* 287 (August 1972), pp. 465–466.

16. Edmund D. Pellegrino, "Humanism in Human Experimentation: Some Notes of the Investigator's Fiduciary Role," *Texas Reports on Biology and Medicine,* 32 (Spring 1974), pp. 311–325.

17. Robert Miller and Henry S. Willner, "Sounding Board: The Two-Part Consent Form," *New England Journal of Medicine* (April 25, 1974), pp. 964–966.

18. Michael Sacks, Edward B. Fink, and William T. Carpenter, "Functioning at the Clinical Research Interface: The Clinical Research Meeting," *American Journal of Psychiatry,* 132 (September 1974), pp. 919–923.

19. Peter F. Woodford, "Ethical Experimentation and the Editor," *New England Journal of Medicine,* 286 (April 20, 1972), p. 892.

20. Eugene G. Laforet, "The Fiction of Informed Consent," *Journal of the American Medical Association,* 235 (April 12, 1976), pp. 1579 and 1584.

21. Pellegrino, op. cit., p. 318.

9

Family Violence: An Issue of the 1980s

Carolyn Kott Washburne

Social workers whose practice focuses on families cannot help but know that family violence is a significant problem in the United States. One research report after another documents that incidents of child abuse and neglect, spouse abuse, substance abuse, sibling abuse, and abuse of the elderly are increasing or, if not increasing, are becoming more visible. Newspapers, magazines, radio, and television have brought the message about family violence to the general public. Professional publications have begun to emphasize that spouse abuse or child abuse is often not the only difficulty occurring in a family, that many families experience more than one of these problems either simultaneously or separately. Educators and practitioners in the human services are communicating with each other at conferences and in professional journals about the complexity of these interrelated problems and the difficulty of finding or implementing viable solutions. It appears that the family, considered by most people to be a haven of warmth, security, and love, may be the most conflict-ridden institution in the country. In an often repeated quote, Straus said before a United States Senate subcommittee, "Violence occurs between family members more often than it occurs in any other setting except with armies in war and police during riots."[1]

Family violence is an issue social workers must deal with if for no other reason than that they come upon it so often in social work practice. Violent families require services from hospitals, protective services agencies, family service agencies, substance abuse counseling programs, the courts, the public schools, and shelters for battered women—all settings in which social workers practice. Most practitioners agree that the resources now available to them to help these families are inadequate. One challenge of the 1980s for all human service professionals is to develop the knowledge base and treatment skills necessary to work effectively with violent families.

The premises on which this article is based are that family violence is a serious problem in the United States and that the various manifestations of family violence must be recognized not as separate issues, but as interrelated symptoms of the same problem if prevention and intervention efforts are to be successful. After an overview of the problem and a look at the interrelationships among its various aspects, the article discusses (1) the difficulties in working with the problem of family violence, (2) possible long-range and short-term solutions to the problem, and (3) the critical role that the profession of social work and social workers as individuals can play in bringing about these solutions.

Scope of the Problem

Although in the 1970s there was an upsurge of public and professional attention to family violence, the problem is as old as humankind. The maltreatment of children, for example, can be traced to the beginnings of recorded history and, if we are to believe the Bible and mythology, to prerecorded history.[2] Child abandonment and infanticide have been accepted practice in various cultures for centuries. The abuse of women also has a long history. The word "family" comes from the Roman word *familia,* which denoted the slaves belonging to an individual. A man's family was considered part of his property, to do with as he wished, a concept that contributed to the Judeo-Christian legacy of women's inferiority and a husband's right to "chastise" his wife at will.[3]

In the United States, concern about family violence, particularly about the maltreatment of children, and legal measures to check it, date back to colonial times, but public and professional concern about the problem has become especially intense in the last two decades. Child abuse was "discovered" in the early 1960s by pediatric radiologists; concern for the problem then spread beyond the medical community to social and governmental agencies and to the mass media, especially after the enactment of the Child Abuse Prevention and Treatment Act of 1974. The focus on the abuse of women was prompted by public outcry from feminists in the early 1970s. Grassroots women's groups began providing such services as counseling and shelters to meet the obvious need. State and local legislation to support these services and mandate legal reforms has been enacted in the past few years, and federal legislation is pending. Other aspects of family violence—sibling abuse, abuse of the elderly, and substance abuse as it affects violent family interactions—have also received professional and public attention.

How widespread is family violence? Researchers agree the problem is extensive but do not frequently agree on the numbers. Reviewing research, Steinmetz found there are 47 million married couples in the United States; based on data samples, it is estimated that 3.3 million wives and over a quarter of a million husbands have experienced severe beatings from their spouses. This excludes beatings by a nonmarried partner or by a former spouse. Spouses kill each other, too; different studies reveal that between 13 and 23 percent of all homicides occur between spouses. One study showed that 24.7 percent of all homicide victims and offenders were members of the same family.[4]

Probably the most prevalent form of family violence is parent-child violence, primarily because corporal punishment is such a widely accepted form of discipline in this country. Surveys have shown that between 84 and 97 percent of all parents have physically punished their child at some time. It has been suggested that corporal punishment and child abuse are on the same continuum.[5] Estimates of the extensiveness of child abuse range from between six thousand and half a million incidents a year. Two thousand children were killed by their parents in 1975. In 1977, there were an estimated ten million alcoholics in the United States, and of the validated cases of child abuse and neglect that year, alcohol dependence was officially considered a factor in 17 percent of the cases.[6] Other studies suggest that this figure is much higher, between 30 and 50 percent. There are only a few studies of sibling abuse and the abuse of the elderly, but what is known indicates that these, too, are widespread and need to be studied further. Although the literature contains controversies about whether family violence is more prevalent in working-class and poor families than in other segments of society, it is safe to say that family violence occurs in middle-class families as well as working-class and poor families.

Numerous secondary problems have been linked to family violence, but little research exists to validate these connections empirically. Individuals involved in nonfamilial murder, political assassination, prostitution, and adolescent homicide often come from violent families.[7]

Articles concerning the theoretical, policy, program, and practice implications of family violence are abundant in the literature, indicating that the problem is a significant one for a broad range of human service professionals.[8]

The various manifestations of family violence are interrelated and must be viewed as such if prevention and treatment efforts are to be successful and if the research is to be meaningful. Specialized knowledge about a particular aspect of the problem is important, but it is also essential to maintain a recognition of the whole. Nearly any practitioner who works with violent families has observed that these families often exhibit more than one kind of violent behavior and that the different kinds of violence influence one another. The research has yet to document this phenomenon, but it has revealed some strong correlations. Several studies have shown that alcohol abuse directly correlates with the abuse of women; it appears that men use their drinking as an excuse to beat their women rather than beat them because they have lost control while drunk.[9]

The relationship between alcohol abuse and child abuse is more complicated. Studies indicate that alcoholic parents are more likely to abuse or neglect their children than the general population, but other factors contribute to the abuse.[10] It is difficult to separate the effects of the addiction from other stresses on abusive families, stresses that often include poverty, family disruption, abuse of the parent as a child, and psychological disorders. One study indicated that substance abuse may deter a potentially abusive parent; many of the fathers in the study deliberately avoided their children when drinking because they feared becoming violent with them.[11]

Another issue that needs further study is the extent to which violent behavior is perpetuated in subsequent generations of the same family. There is considerable evidence that many abusive parents were abused themselves as children; there is also evidence that a high percentage of battered women witnessed the abuse of their own mothers when they were young. The family, because it is the primary socializing institution in this country, can be a training ground for violence. However, it is important not to assume that violent behavior will be passed on in families. This is not true in all families, and individuals have the capacity to overcome even the most damaging family environments.[12] To what extent families pass on violent tendencies, how the various forms of family violence interconnect, and what can be done to break these cycles await further research.

Difficult Problem

Even when there is acknowledgment of the complexity and inter-relatedness of the various aspects of family violence, solutions do not immediately become obvious. Current efforts to ameliorate the problem have been only occasionally and partially successful, if that. This section of the article outlines the major difficulties encountered by policymakers, activists, and practitioners who are working to improve the lives of violent families. These difficulties include (1) the lack of a national family policy, particularly one that supports families' inherent coping abilities, (2) the lack of an adequate knowledge base, (3) the tendency of research studies and treatment approaches to erroneously presume that abusive families are pathological, and (4) the obstacles created by interagency and interdisciplinary conflicts.

Lack of a National Policy   The United States does not have an explicit national family policy. When he was campaigning for the presidency, Jimmy Carter said, "It is clear that the national government should have a strong profamily policy, but the fact is that our government has no family policy, and that is the same as an antifamily policy."[13] Although there is a plethora of political rhetoric about the importance of the family as the cornerstone of this society, the contradictory hodgepodge of public policies and programs affecting families does more to undermine family strength than to enhance it. As one advisory committee on child development stated,

> Public policies in many areas have effects, both positive and negative, on the welfare of families. Despite this fact, little explicit attention is given to the impact on families and children of welfare, health, housing, transportation, environmental regulation, criminal justice, recreation, consumer protection, and other programs, both old and new.[14]

Programs are not revised quickly enough to accommodate rapidly changing family structures and life-styles. Social security, for example, was created when most married women did not work outside the home and were economically dependent on their husbands. However, more and more families today contain two wage earners, and, in effect, the social security system penalizes these families.[15] Families are expected to take care of their own problems, and those who seek outside help are often stigmatized. Intervention occurs only after a family situation has reached crisis proportions. The lack of a supportive family policy particularly affects vulnerable families whose coping resources, both financial and emotional, are often already stretched to the point where a crisis, even a minor one, can destroy the family's equilibrium.

Sometimes there are specific conflicts between various federal policies or between federal and state policies, and these conflicts hamper practitioners who work with at-risk families. For example, although in some child abuse or neglect cases substance abuse is a contributing factor, most communities have little coordination between the protective services agency and counseling programs for alcoholism and drug abuse. One reason for this is that there is an apparent conflict between the federal statutes and regulations which protect the confidentiality of the records of alcohol and drug abuse patients and the state laws which require reporting by certain professionals of suspected child abuse and neglect cases. A substance abuse counselor, therefore, may be reluctant to report a suspected case for fear not only of violating agency policy, but also of undermining the therapeutic relationship with the client.

Inadequate Knowledge Base Although the recent proliferation of publications about family violence suggests that academicians and practitioners are quite knowledgeable about the problem, the reality is that information about its extent, causes, and remedies is limited. In 1979, Zigler wrote, "There is general agreement that theoretical and empirical research in the area of child abuse remains primitive and rudimentary. The work done to date has been relatively recent, relatively limited in quantity, and poor in quality."[16] Another article suggests that "few attempts are made to bridge the gap between qualitative and quantitative research. One consequence is that generalizations are often repeated ad infinitum until they assume the stature of fact."[17] Research about spouse abuse, sibling abuse, and the abuse of the elderly is in an even more embryonic stage. Although the existence of plentiful, high-quality research about family violence will not guarantee that sound policies will be formulated or effective treatment programs developed, before progress can be made on a large scale it will be necessary to understand the nature of the problem and the successes and failures of previous efforts to solve it.

One reason for the scarcity of good research is that the subject has been investigated only for a relatively short time. Another reason is that it is difficult to research complex human interactions, especially ones that are considered deviant. Some of the specific inadequacies of the research data are that (1) much of it is based on cases which have come to the attention of public agencies, leading to an overrepresentation of poor and minority families, (2) much of the research has been based on self-reports, so that violent families which are still "in the closet" are not included, (3) many of the research samples have been small, regional, and nonrepresentative, (4) there are methodological difficulties even in defining violence and then in quantifying information about it, and (5) it is awkward and potentially inflammatory to interview a family about its violent behavior.[18]

Presumptions of Pathology   Another deficiency in the research on family violence is that it is rarely based on the observations of practitioners and is usually not geared to their needs. Practitioners are forced to rely on irrelevant or erroneous information about how to work with violent families. One questionable but nonetheless widespread approach is rooted in the pathology of the individual family. Most experts in the field believe that only about 10 percent of the abusive parents are seriously disturbed, yet much of the research, and the treatment approaches based on this research, continues to focus on the presumed pathology.[19]

Although it is beyond the scope of this article to discuss the various theories about the causes of family violence, the author concurs with those researchers and theoreticians who posit multidimensional models. Gelles, for example, disputes the idea that there is one cause of child abuse—mental illness—and argues that there are many causal factors, including the social context of the family, family roles, and economic stress.[20] Activists in the movement against the abuse of women also take issue with the psychopathological model. Men who beat their wives, they say, are not deviants, but men not too different from the average who are acting out this society's sanctioned oppression of women.[21] Legal remedies or treatment programs based on the assumption that family violence is a disease to be cured are not effective for either intervention or prevention.[22]

Fragmentation of Services   The professional literature in the human services is replete with articles that catalogue the failures of most social service delivery systems in this country; fragmentation, inaccessibility, and nonaccountability are the most frequently mentioned causes of this failure. Violent families seeking help are likely to encounter all these shortcomings and more, particularly because many different types of services may be needed and few, if any, will be found under the same roof. A battered woman, for example, en route from her abusive home to a new life on her own may come in contact with the police, the hospital emergency room, the district attorney's office, the shelter for battered women, the welfare department, and the housing authorities.

If she has children, she may also have contact with protective services and school counselors. Like the blind people feeling the elephant, each of these agencies views this woman's problems from its own perspective, and they probably have little knowledge of the others. Unless she has an advocate to help her negotiate with all these institutions and agencies, the battered woman, who is vulnerable to begin with, is likely to become even more overwhelmed just from the process of getting help for herself.

Even when an agency worker, or perhaps an entire agency, makes an effort to coordinate other services, there are sometimes specific constraints on referrals among agencies in a given community, as mentioned earlier. In addition, there is the problem of interdisciplinary misunderstanding and mistrust. Professionals who work with violent families come from a variety of disciplines and work in a variety of settings. Rarely are they familiar with the functions, ethical issues, problems, or languages of the other disciplines.[23] These disciplinary barriers are sometimes exacerbated when the value orientation of traditional agencies clashes with those of alternative agencies.[24]

Moving toward Solutions

Enumerating these difficulties is in no way meant to suggest that the problem of family violence is insoluble or that more research data are needed before the problem can be tackled. On the contrary, enough information is in hand to enable work to begin on some of the basic changes that need to occur.

Clearly, it is necessary to press for a supportive national policy on families if efforts at the state, community, local, and agency levels are to be effective. Numerous policymakers, academicians, and practitioners have combined their energies on committees and task forces to make recommendations about appropriate policies and programs for families and children. Many of these recommendations are sound; most of them go unimplemented. To create the conditions under which family violence can be eliminated, efforts must first be made to implement those recommendations that address the economic, sexual, and racial inequities in this country.[25] Policies that support the natural helping networks which are already available to families—neighborhood, community, ethnic, family, religious, and self-help networks—are especially worthy of consideration. The creation of a national policy on families must be prefaced by a thorough examination of individual and group values and customs in this country. It may be that to change the attitudes which sanction violence it will be necessary to change cherished values about the privacy of the family.

Better coordination among agencies needs to be another goal. In many cases, if this cooperation is to occur at the local level, federal agencies must provide leadership in developing guidelines that can be implemented locally. One such example is the joint policy statement on the "Confidentiality of Alcohol and Drug Abuse Patient Records and Child Abuse and Neglect Reporting" issued by the Alcohol, Drug Abuse, and Mental Health Administration (ADAMHA) and the National Center of Child Abuse and Neglect (NCCAN).[26] This joint policy statement, along with a model qualified services agreement, specifies the ways in which programs receiving ADAMHA funds are to enter into an agreement with child protective service agencies that will permit the agencies to receive reports of suspected child abuse and neglect in their localities and also insure that the confidentiality of alcohol and drug abuse patient records will be protected. This kind of administrative support is crucial if agency workers are to get the resources they need to work with violent families.

Promoting agency coordination at the community level requires more than a joint policy statement issued by two federal agencies. Among the proposed models for such coordination, those that involve participation by professionals from various disciplines and by citizens are the most promising. The community team approach to child abuse and neglect developed by Helfer is a model that could be adapted to the broader problem of family violence.[27] Such community teams have proved effective in facilitating interagency and interdisciplinary communication, reducing agency turf problems and buck-passing, developing broadly based community support, and raising public consciousness about the issues.[28] They also alleviate the common problem of burnout among staff working on cases in which families are actively or potentially violent.

In communities where such teams are not yet developed or are not feasible, agency personnel can arrange in-service training sessions to familiarize themselves with other programs in the community that work with violent families and to sensitize themselves to issues faced by other disciplines. In-service training can also be held on new research findings and innovative approaches to treatment. Some of the most successful programs for violence-prone families use paraprofessionals, volunteers, and the families' own helping networks.[29] Professionals—line staff, supervisors, and administrators—need to be open to integrating these resources with their own services. Nonprofessionals and

workers in alternative agencies need to be open to working coopera-
tively with other agencies to insure the best services for their clients.

Holistic Approach

If, as some researchers and most activists assert, the typical child abuser
or wife beater is not a psychopath but someone who is acting out this
society's covert and sometimes overt acceptance of violence, then we
social workers must begin our efforts to ameliorate the problem of
family violence by examining our own attitudes toward violence. How
different are we from these families that have been labeled deviant? To
what extent do we tolerate or even encourage violence in our personal
lives? Our professional lives? What are our values and how do we act
them out? We need to look at the ways in which this culture glorifies
and reinforces violent behavior. We need to support programs and
research studies that take into account the social, economic, psychological, biological, legal, and educational aspects of family violence. We
need to push for the widespread implementation of programs that
have already been demonstrated to be successful and cost-efficient.
Although we need to learn more about the problem, we should not
hesitate to speak out about what we already know. It has been established, for example, that child abuse and the abuse of women correlate
with unemployment. Many of the solutions to the problem of family
violence involve political considerations, and we need to integrate
political awareness into our treatment and research.

Social Work Role

Social workers can be a key factor in the effort to eliminate family
violence. The National Association of Social Workers recognized this
potential by including a policy proposal on domestic violence among its
proposals on public issues to be discussed and approved at the 1979
Delegate Assembly.[30] The profession of social work and social workers
as individuals are in a position to demonstrate leadership on this issue
for several reasons. First, since social workers practice in virtually all
the settings where violent families come or are sent for help, it is the
rare social work practitioner who has not come across such a family.
Awareness of the various manifestations of the problem can be an aid
in identifying families who may need additional or specialized services.
Social workers, who are generally oriented to using community resources, are in a good position to assist families get all the services they

need by helping them negotiate their way through the service delivery network. Further, because social work theory is eclectic, social workers tend not to be as locked into a specific perspective as some other professionals and thus have the ability to facilitate the interdisciplinary coordination and cooperation that is essential in this field. Because some social work treatment methods have emphasized family systems and have favored a holistic rather than a pathological orientation to family dynamics, social workers have a head start in understanding and working effectively with violent families.

Finally, social workers need to draw on the profession's legacy of activism and community involvement to round out the multifaceted approach needed for dealing with the problem of family violence. The professional association can encourage training on family violence for practitioners. Schools of social work can develop curricula that will prepare graduates for the realities of working with violent families. Individual social workers can become aware of their responsibility to influence policies related to families and children. This last is especially important. Some social workers, especially those with a treatment orientation, have tended to view policy issues as outside their area of concern or expertise. Yet it is precisely this first-hand knowledge of families that needs to be incorporated into policy formulation and program development. Social work and social workers have already been active in this way. The American Public Welfare Association and the National Association of Social Workers, through a grant from NCCAN, have established a National Professional Resource Center on Child Abuse and Neglect in Washington, D.C. Social workers as individuals and as representatives of the professional association have testified on proposed legislation related to domestic violence.[31] Social work involvement in advisory boards at the community, state, and national levels is important. Social work input into the pending congressional legislation to develop domestic violence treatment and research projects is crucial.

Family violence is widespread in this country, and it is a multidimensional problem. That the topic has become fashionable should not diminish its seriousness. The physical and emotional suffering of persons who live in violent families is immeasurable. The financial costs of foster care, penal and psychiatric incarceration, and rehabilitation services, to mention a few of the costs that arise out of family violence, are borne by everyone. So are the emotional costs of living in a society in which violence against people and property is a daily reality. Family violence is a problem that deserves the utmost professional concern.

Notes and References

1. *Milwaukee Sentinel,* February 15, 1978, p. 2.

2. Naomi Feigelson Chase, *A Child is Being Beaten* (New York: McGraw-Hill Book Co., 1975), p. 8.

3. Del Martin, *Battered Wives* (San Francisco: Glide Publications, 1976), p. 25.

4. Suzanne K. Steinmetz, "Violence between Family Members," *Marriage and Family Review,* 1 (May–June 1978), pp. 1–16.

5. *See,* for example, Norma D. Feshbach, "The Effects of Violence in Childhood," in David G. Gil, ed., *Child Abuse and Violence* (New York: AMS Press, 1979), pp. 575–585.

6. *National Analysis of Official Child Neglect and Abuse Reporting: An Executive Summary* (Denver, Colo.: American Humane Association, 1977), p. 5.

7. "Report of the Special Populations Subpanel on the Mental Health of Women," *Task Panel Reports Submitted to the President's Commission on Mental Health,* Vol. 3 (Washington, D.C.: U.S. Government Printing Office, 1978), p. 104.

8. Mary Hanemann Lystad, "Violence at Home: A Review of the Literature," *American Journal of Orthopsychiatry,* 45 (April 1975), pp. 328–345.

9. Steinmetz, op. cit., p. 8.

10. Margaret Hindman, "Child Abuse and Neglect: The Alcohol Connection," *Alcohol Health and Research World,* (Spring 1977), pp. 2–7.

11. Joseph Mayer, Rebecca Black, and James MacDonall, "An Investigation of Relationships among Substance Abuse, Child Care, and Child Abuse/Neglect." Paper presented at the Fifty-fourth Annual Meeting of the American Orthopsychiatric Association, New York, April 1977.

12. Maya Pines, "Superkids," *Psychology Today,* 12 (January 1979), pp. 53–63.

13. *Strengthening Families through Informal Support Systems,* report of a Wingspread Conference (Racine, Wis.: The Johnson Foundation, 1979), p. 1.

14. Advisory Committee on Child Development, Assembly of Behavioral and Social Sciences, National Research Council, *Toward a National Policy for Children and Families* (Washington, D.C.: National Academy of Sciences), pp. 4–5.

15. Susan Dworkin, "Notes on Carter's Family Policy—How It Got That Way," *Ms. Magazine,* 6 (September 1978), p. 61.

16. Edward Zigler, "Controlling Child Abuse in America: An Effort Doomed to Failure," in Gil, op. cit., p. 38.

17. Lillian Pike Cain and Lorraine V. Klerman, "What Do Social Workers Read about Child Abuse?" *Child Welfare,* 57 (January 1979), p. 22.

18. Richard J. Gelles, "How Violent Are American Families," in Carolyn

Kott Washburne, Thomas R. Bell, and Adrienne Ahlgren Haeuser, *Family Violence: Can We Prevent It?* Unpublished manuscript, Milwaukee, 1978.

19. National Center on Child Abuse and Neglect, *Child Abuse and Neglect: The Problem and Its Management,* Vol. 1 (Washington, D.C.: U.S. Government Printing Office, 1975), p. 12.

20. Richard J. Gelles, "Child Abuse as Psychopathology: A Sociological Critique and Reformulation," in Gil, ed., op. cit., pp. 49–65.

21. *See,* for example, *Battered Women: Issues of Public Policy,* (Washington, D.C.: U.S. Commission on Civil Rights, 1978).

22. Richard J. Gelles, "Child Abuse as Psychopathology," p. 62.

23. For an example of an attempt to remedy these disparities, *see* National Center on Child Abuse and Neglect, *Interdisciplinary Glossary on Child Abuse and Neglect: Legal, Medical, Social Work Terms,* (Washington, D.C.: U.S. Government Printing Office, 1978).

24. For a discussion of some of these issues, *see* Claudette McShane, "Community Services for Battered Women," *Social Work,* 24 (January 1979), pp. 34–39; and Miriam Galper and Carolyn Kott Washburne, "Maximizing the Impact of an Alternative Agency," *Journal of Sociology and Social Welfare,* 55 (November 1976), pp. 248–257.

25. See, for example, any of the works of David G. Gil, *Violence against Children* (Cambridge, Mass.: Harvard University Press, 1970), *Unravelling Social Policy* and *The Challenge of Social Equality* (Cambridge, Mass.: Schenkman Publishing Co., 1973 and 1976, respectively), and *Child Abuse and Violence.*

26. Alcohol, Drug Abuse, and Mental Health Administration and National Center on Child Abuse and Neglect, "Confidentiality of Drug and Alcohol Patient Records and Child Abuse and Neglect Reporting," Joint Policy Statement (Washington, D.C.: Department of Health, Education and Welfare, February 1, 1978).

27. National Center on Child Abuse and Neglect, *The Problem and Its Management,* Vol. 3 (Washington, D.C.: U.S. Government Printing Office, 1975).

28. Adrienne Abhlgren Haeuser, "Community Participation in the Prevention and Treatment of Child Abuse and Neglect," *Volunteer Administration,* 10 (Spring 1977), pp. 15–21.

29. *Executive Summary: Evaluation of the Joint OCD/SRS National Demonstration Program in Child Abuse and Neglect, 1974–1977* (Berkeley, Calif.: Berkeley Planning Associates, December 1977). (Mimeographed.)

30. "Delegate Assembly—Time of Decision Nears," *NASW News,* 24 (July 1979), p. 18.

31. *See,* for example, Elizabeth Davoren, testimony on behalf of the National Association of Social Workers, *Hearings before the Subcommittee on Child and Human Development, Committee on Human Resources* (Washington, D.C.: U.S. Government Printing Office, 1978), pp. 268–278.

10

Running: The New Therapy

Richard L. Edwards,
Ben P. Granger,
and Bruce W. Guillaume

Running has been described as the nation's latest growth industry, and it is estimated that more than 25 million Americans now run or jog on a reasonably regular basis.[1] Running has captured the attention of the business world, the media, and the general public. It has also become the subject of an increasing amount of research. The attention of researchers in both the physical and social sciences is a welcome development because, as Andersen pointed out,

> as running becomes more popular, it suffers the growing pains of any phenomenon. It polarizes the public. There seems to be no one left in America neutral on the subject of running. You either see it as a madness that can do nothing short of ruining every American who takes part in it, or you see it as the cure-all for every possible ailment that could afflict an American, from the common cold to cancer.[2]

In reality, it is likely that running will neither lead to the ruination of American society nor be a panacea for all individual and collective problems. Sound research that sheds light on the actual benefits of running will help to separate fact from fantasy. Reports of such research have begun to be published in a variety of professional journals, and so far studies on the physiological effects of running have been more numerous than those on the psychological or psychosocial effects.

Although various explanations have been offered for the running

craze, recent research suggests that a major factor in the phenomenon
may be the positive psychosocial effects that running has on individuals.[3] Some mental health researchers carry this notion a step further
and suggest that not only does running have potential psychosocial
benefits, but that it can actually be used as a valuable part of a therapeutic approach to various mental health disorders.[4]

The use of running in psychotherapeutic or counseling processes is a
radical concept because it carries with it some assumptions that, if
accepted, require basic or radical changes in the traditional medical-
model approaches that dominate mental health practice. Although research on running and its relationship to mental health is increasing,
the research to date has been carried out primarily by psychiatrists and
psychologists. A search of the social work literature reveals no published studies on the use of running in the therapeutic helping process.
Because social workers deliver such a significant proportion of the
mental health services, it is important for social workers to become
familiar with new, and even radical, developments that are studied and
advocated by their colleagues in related mental health disciplines. The
research on running and mental health published thus far suggests that
running can be efficacious in the treatment of such conditions as
depression and anxiety. Therefore, it can be expected that mental
health practitioners who are eager to try that which works will begin to
use running as a therapeutic technique in the 1980s.

The purpose of this article is to inform social workers about the
current status of research on running's effects on mental health, to
provide some examples of ways in which running can be incorporated
into treatment plans, and to identify indicators and contraindicators for
the use of running as an adjunct to therapeutic intervention.

Overview of the Research

The literature concerning the human body's physiological responses to
vigorous exercise is extensive, and it leaves little doubt that exercise is
beneficial and necessary in maintaining health, promoting growth, and
perhaps even in retarding the aging process. The heart rate, respira-
tion rate, hormone levels, blood chemistry, and most other bodily
functions are positively affected by exercise, and prolonged exercise
has been found to have a significant positive effect on the cardiovascular system. Cardiovascular fitness is commonly viewed as a prime indicator of physical well-being.[5] Furthermore, research conducted by
Kasch at the San Diego State University Exercise Physiology Laboratory

revealed that an experimental group of middle-aged men who, for a ten-year period, participated regularly in either running or swimming showed no signs of increasing age in any of four major indicators.[6]

Although the literature on the physiological benefit of running is extensive, it is only recently that evidence has become available to show that exercise affects the emotional or psychosocial state of individuals. Much of this research is anecdotal, but the professional literature has recently begun to include reports of controlled experiments that link exercise in general, and running in particular, to positive psychosocial changes.

In 1973, Ismail and Trachtman reported a study of sixty middle-aged men, all employees of Purdue University, who were involved in an exercise program of four months' duration that included running an average of two to three miles a day. Testing revealed that as the participants in this exercise program became more physically fit, they also became more open and extroverted, more relaxed, and more stable and self-confident.[7] Orwin reported a successful therapeutic program that used running as a major component in treating eight agoraphobic patients. He suggested that the running inhibited the patients' anxiety in several ways:

1. An instinctive response to anxiety—that is, rapid, forceful action—was used to control it.
2. The ongoing autonomic excitation caused by vigorous physical activity competed with and inhibited the anxiety reaction, allowing appreciation of the environment without awareness of fear.
3. If any autonomic component of the anxiety reaction could be detected it would be cognitively labelled as part of the body's response to physical exercise.[8]

There are some anecdotal reports on the successful use of running in the treatment of both anorexia nervosa and schizophrenia, but the sizes of the samples make it impossible to generalize.[9] The bulk of the research on the psychosocial impact of running has focused on the linkage between running and either depression or anxiety. Large-scale population surveys have found that depression is the most common psychiatric disorder in the United States.[10] It is widespread in American society, and it is the form of psychopathology most frequently seen by physicians. Furthermore, depression appears to underlie many physical complaints. Suicide, which in many instances represents an extreme reaction to depression, has become the second most common cause of death of adolescents.[11]

Anxiety neurosis is another major mental health problem in the

United States and is probably second only to depression in its inci-
dence. It has been estimated that ten million Americans suffer from
anxiety neurosis and that as many as 30 percent of all patients seen by
general practitioners are anxiety neurotics. Many more patients suffer
from conditions that have their origin in unrelieved stress.[12]

Research has shown running to be a significant factor in relieving
depression and anxiety. Post and Goodwin noted improvements in
moderately depressed patients who adopted a program of regular
exercise.[13] Folkin et al. found that after participating in a semester-long
jogging course, a sample of college women were less depressed than
they had been previously.[14]

Brown, Ramirez, and Taub studied about seven hundred subjects,
including a number of depressed persons, who began a variety of
programs of regular physical exercise such as jogging, swimming,
walking, and tennis. The study revealed that persons who were free of
dysphoric moods reported a feeling of well-being associated with exercise, that exercise was effective in warding off the depressed and
pessimistic moods that mentally healthy people often experience, and
that depressed persons of widely differing ages became less depressed
and less anxious when they achieved a state of physical fitness. Depression scores decreased among those who engaged in wrestling, mixed
exercises, jogging, and tennis, but not in those who participated in
softball and not in the control group who had no exercise routine.
Jogging five days a week during a ten-week period was associated with
significant reductions in the depression scores of both depressed and
nondepressed subjects. Similar patterns were exhibited by those who
jogged only three days per week, although the degree of change in
their depression scores was not as great.[15]

Greist et al. studied running as a form of treatment for depressed
psychiatric outpatients.[16] They randomly assigned patients to one of
the three types of treatment programs: time-limited psychotherapy (ten
sessions), time-unlimited psychotherapy, and individual running with a
leader who had no training in psychotherapy. Patients assigned to the
running program met with the running leader three times a week for
thirty to forty-five minutes each session. There was no discussion of
depression; the focus was on aspects of running. Analysis of the results
of this study revealed that the patients assigned to the running program had a rapid and high degree of improvement compared to the
patients assigned to either of the two psychotherapy programs. A
follow-up study showed that the improvement in those assigned to the

running program persisted for two years after the completion of the original study.

Murphy et al. studied the effects of exercise on alcoholics and found that they reported less depression and anxiety as their physical fitness improved.[17] Powell reported that institutionalized geriatric patients assigned to an exercise group showed significant improvement on two of three cognitive tests compared to patients assigned to a social group and a control group.[18]

Research on the effects of exercise on anxiety has demonstrated that exercise does result in a decrease in anxiety, but the exercise must be vigorous to have an influence.[19] Sime reported that light exercise does not modify anxiety, and this supports conclusions drawn earlier by Morgan et al.[20] In other research, Morgan and Horstman found that vigorous walking and running resulted in biochemical changes that were associated with significant decreases in anxiety for both normal and clinically anxious subjects.[21]

Some research has indicated that exercise may be more effective in reducing tension than medication. De Vries and Adams studied a group of people between the ages of 52 and 70 who complained of nervous tension, sleeplessness, irritability, continual worry, and feelings of panic in everyday situations. The researchers tested the subjects after administering four hundred milligrams of meprobamate, a tranquilizer; after administering an identical-looking placebo; and after the subjects engaged in periods of exercise. They found that the exercise was more effective in reducing tension than either the tranquilizer or the placebo.[22]

In summary, then, the available research suggests that exercise in general, and running in particular, is associated with decreases in anxiety and depression. The exercise must be vigorous to be beneficial, and running appears to be more effective than other forms of exercise. Running has been found to help participants become more open, relaxed, and self-confident, and some of the research suggests that running may be a viable alternative to medication for some patients.

Psychosocial Effects of Running

Research to explain why running has positive psychosocial effects is not conclusive, but there are a number of theories available. Greist et al. suggest that various components of running are helpful to different individuals:

1. Biochemical changes [are] associated with physical activity . . ., and it seems probable that the sensation of feeling better is mediated by brain norepinephrine or other amine neurotransmitters (or perhaps the recently discovered morphine-like endorphins) which may be regulated toward a more normal functional state by physical activity.

2. The freedom and the renewed capacity to think creatively on most runs greatly relieves persons who have been mired in depressive ruminations. A depression-free interlude on the run, even if short-lived, renews hope that the illness itself will be time-limited.

3. Runners at all levels constantly experience new and real bodily sensations, and knowing that these sensations originate in the running experience can be a great relief for a depressed person troubled by minor but annoying somatic complaints.

4. Patients who become runners can develop a sense of mastery of what should be considered a difficult skill. . . .[23]

Andersen, who approaches depression from a psychoanalytic viewpoint, defining it as anger turned inward and suggesting that it usually relates to some sort of loss, sees running as an effective adjunct to the treatment of depression. He believes running is a means of draining off some of the anger the individual feels over the loss.[24]

Running generally results in a significant increase in overall physical fitness, and this, in turn, often leads to an increase in self-esteem. Running also enables participants to exercise a maximum of self-control, which can have a positive effect on depression. The participant chooses the time, place, and duration of a run and can experience success in a variety of ways. For many persons, the ability to run half a mile, a mile, or longer distances is intrinsically rewarding.

Theories explaining the effects of running on anxiety are similar to those offered to explain its effects on depression. Running is thought to have a calming or tranquilizing effect, and the effort involved in running seems to drain off tension. Bahrke and Morgan approach the matter from a different perspective, suggesting that diversion may be the crucial ingredient in leading to decreased anxiety. They found that subjects who engaged in quiet rest in a sound-filtered room all experienced significant decreases in anxiety. They concluded that running permits participants to "drift away from the concerns of the day" and, as a consequence, to become deeply relaxed.[25]

Andersen suggests that running is a relaxing activity, a kind of natural tranquilizer. He believes anxiety relates to relaxation inversely, but that relaxation is frequently elusive when it is most needed. Andersen further suggests that although individuals cannot command themselves to relax, they can facilitate the process by taking specific steps to deal with the problem that is causing the anxiety. This can be done either indirectly, by engaging in some activity that distracts attention from the problem, or directly, by engaging in problem-solving activity. He suggests that running can be an effective means to do both:

> 1. Running reduces tension by enabling the individual to take his/her mind off the problem for a while. Further, the easy, rhythmic activity of running has a soothing quality.
> 2. Running is an aid to problem-solving because it allows for a variety of imputed meanings and it allows for a form of regression which occurs when the individual begins, during a run, to revert feelings, actions, and behavior to a state of being more nearly like that experienced at an early age. In other words, during the running experience the individual may begin to feel more acutely and think less acutely, to engage in primary process thinking which is characterized by a decrease in logic, a loss of time perspective, increased use of symbols and fluidity of attention. This experience of primary process thinking, Andersen believes, can lead to increased creativity and a better capacity for problem solving, as well as renewed energy.[26]

Both Kostrabula and Glasser have theorized that running may have positive psychological effects because of its tendency to result in what they have labeled a "positive addiction."[27] They suggest that prolonged running, as well as certain other kinds of activities, such as transcendental meditation, cycling, and swimming, can have addictive qualities of a positive nature that can strengthen the individual and lead to a more productive and rewarding life.

It is clear that more research is needed to clarify why running seems to have positive psychosocial effects. However, the continued search for clearcut answers should not preclude the use of running in the treatment of problems that are troubling large numbers of individuals in American society. Of the various forms of treatment currently used to deal with depressed and anxious clients, there is little research to demonstrate their efficacy or to explain why they work, if they do. One consideration about running as a form of or aid to psychosocial treatment is that not only does the research indicate that running is helpful; it is also clear that running often produces beneficial side effects, such as cardiovascular fitness, weight loss, improved pulmonary functions, and overall fitness, that justify its advocacy even in the absence of clear proof of an antidepressant or anxiety-reducing effect.

Running as Intervention

It is reasonable to ask why, if one decides to use some form of exercise as a component of psychotherapy or counseling, should running be the exercise chosen? There are a variety of reasons. Running has been shown to be superior to other forms of exercise in its impact on depression and anxiety.[28] Running is an exercise that requires no special equipment other than a pair of running shoes and can be engaged in almost any time and place; it is thus not an activity available only to the middle or upper class. Running does not require any special skill or athletic ability, and participants who have never done well at team sports can be successful at running. Unlike team sports, running is usually noncompetitive and allows the individual to benefit from participation without the pressures of worrying about winning or losing. For many runners, the ability to run a particular distance is extremely gratifying.

Although the use of running in the process of psychosocial treatment is in an embryonic stage, a number of approaches are beginning to emerge. These can be broadly divided into individual or group processes, with running either as the sole form of treatment or combined with traditional interventive methods.

One of the first therapists to use running as an adjunct to traditional psychotherapy was Kostrabula, a psychiatrist, who established closed groups of outpatients composed of persons of both sexes with a wide range of presenting problems. Kostrabula's groups met with him three times a week for approximately two hours. The first hour was spent running and walking, and the second hour was devoted to discussion. These groups were viewed by Kostrabula as highly successful.[29]

The authors have experienced success with two variations of Kostrabula's model. In one, the clients met weekly with the therapist for a group running session and were encouraged to run on their own between the group sessions. The group sessions did not include any period of discussion following the running. This approach worked particularly well with a group of college-age youths who experienced increased self-esteem and self-confidence and decreased anxiety as a result of their running therapy. In another variation of Kostrabula's model, one of the authors used group running in combination with individual therapy.

Kostrabula and others have also used running in conjunction with individual therapy. This is done in various ways: the client's problems can be discussed during the running session; the individual running sessions with the therapist can be held in addition to more traditional individual therapy or counseling sessions; or the client can be encouraged to use running time for mental rehearsal or problem-solving activity.

One of the authors is currently using running with approximately one-third of his clients, either as the primary form of intervention or in conjunction with more traditional forms of intervention. The clients, few of whom are middle-class, respond well to this form of intervention. A Title XX contract monitor, although she acknowledges that the clients have improved during their running therapy, has indicated that she does not consider running a "recognized" form of counseling and thus does not believe it should be eligible for Title XX reimbursement. In contrast, the author's continued use of running has been supported by his colleagues, his supervisor, and the agency's directors, all of whom are impressed by the positive results that are observable in the clients.

Ideally, when running is used as a form of therapy, the therapist runs with the clients. In this way, the therapist can be a positive role model. However, health problems on the part of the therapist or other considerations may make this impossible. In these situations, the therapist may refer clients for assistance in beginning a sound running program. Many high school and college noncredit evening programs are now offering beginning jogging classes, as do many YMCAs and similar organizations. The therapist could also have an experienced runner help a group of clients begin a sound running program and fit this in with the regular counseling sessions.

Although dropout rates between 30 and 70 percent are commonly reported for nontherapy jogging groups, Greist et al. reported only a 10 percent dropout rate for individuals who engaged in running as a prescribed form of therapy for depression.[30]

It is crucial that the therapist follow certain rules in prescribing running as part of the therapeutic process. First, any client over 35 or who seems to have a health problem should be referred to a physician for a thorough physical examination before engaging in a running program. Second, running, like any other form of intervention, should be based on a thorough psychosocial assessment. Third, clients for whom running is recommended must volunteer to engage in the activity; they cannot be forced to run. Fourth, the therapist should be well versed in running literature and should be committed to the notion that the running must be enjoyable for the client.[31] Fifth, the social work adage of "starting where the client is" must be kept in mind. This means that the client who has not run before will need to start slowly. For many clients, this may mean weeks of walking before undertaking any running, and then the running may be interspersed with walking. A basic rule of thumb is that if an individual cannot talk reasonably comfortably while running, the person is running too fast.

In the beginning, it is important to be certain that clients stay well within these physical limits and finish the workout refreshed and looking forward to the next run.

The authors adhere to some basic guidelines in selecting running as part of a treatment plan. Running should not be related to the client's work activities, and the run should be vigorous enough so that the client is slightly out of breath and perspiring mildly at the completion. Competition, at least initially, should be discouraged. The full psychosocial therapeutic benefits of running tend to accrue in noncompetitive situations. However, competitive running may be appropriate in some instances.

The following are case examples of clients treated by one of the authors:

Case 1

A 36-year-old, white female came to the agency complaining of being "sad, depressed, and crying all the time," for three years. Soon after the onset of these complaints, she sought relief and began psychotherapy with a private therapist. As her troublesome behavior became more frequent and increasingly intense, she sought treatment with other counselors. She found no relief for her complaints and was eventually hospitalized for "chronic depression" for one year. She reported a slight decrease in her misery during hospitalization, "but as soon as I got out, I was right back to the same old thing." Except for prescribed medication, she was essentially untreated for six months. At that time, she also began to experience "anxiety attacks—I would get real scared. I hated to be left alone, I would get so nervous I would shake all over."

She then contacted a family service agency. She was given instructions to keep a log of all anxiety-provoking or depressing situations. This assignment was given over a two-week period. She was then introduced to the running program. During the third week, she was given permission to begin daily jogging. She was instructed to maintain her anxiety-depression log. Attempts were made to increase her weekly mileage, although this was not emphasized or done consistently. After four weeks of daily jogging, she began to report relief from her "anxiety attacks" and "depression." Her anxiety-depression log also documented this. She was then instructed to discontinue jogging for two weeks. With that, her log indicated an increase in "anxiety attacks" as well as depression—"a terrible two weeks," she reported. She resumed daily jogging and again the symptoms were reduced. With her doctor's approval, she also began to decrease her antidepressant medication.

It should be noted that during these first three months she had weekly sessions with the worker. The sessions consisted of answering questions about running or taking care of the weekly problems that runners have ("What do you do for a pulled muscle, what kind of shoes should I wear?"). No time was spent talking about events other than running. After three months of weekly sessions, she was given bimonthly appointments and would run with the worker during her meetings. After four such meetings, she was terminated with the knowledge that she could return for "coaching sessions" whenever she desired. When she did not call for "coaching sessions" in six weeks, she was contacted, and she reported that she was continuing to run, had not had any "anxiety attacks," had gotten a job, enjoyed the time she spent with her daughter, and her daughter had begun jogging with her. In addition, she had invested in a rather expensive pair of running shoes and was busy researching the subject of running on her own.

Case 2

A 26-year-old, white, slightly obese female came to the agency complaining that "things are falling down all around me; I'm so nervous I can't stand it and I cry almost all the time." She was referred to the agency by a friend, and this was her first attempt to alleviate her symptoms. She had been depressed/anxious for approximately six months before she sought treatment. At the time she presented herself to the agency, she had filed for a divorce from her husband, who had been somewhat abusive of her in the past. Her divorce hearing was scheduled for two months from the day she began counseling. Information gathered during the initial interview revealed that she perceived ridding herself of the current depressive/anxious symptoms as the top priority of counseling. Issues surrounding the divorce were to be handled "later" and "on my own."

She was asked to record all situations that appeared to cause her depressed or anxious feelings and to return with this information in two weeks. This baseline revealed that she was experiencing depressed/anxious feelings several times daily. The possibility of utilizing a running program was explored with her, and an agreement was reached during the second session. She was shown some basic stretching exercises and instructed to perform these daily. She was instructed to continue monitoring, in writing, her depressive/anxious episodes until her next session, one week later. Upon her return for the third session, her affect was much improved and she reported feeling "much happier and a lot less nervous."

The third session was spent talking about running, answering any questions she had, and actually taking a quarter-mile jog. She was instructed to begin jogging daily. The next four sessions were spent the same way except that increasingly longer distances were utilized. Her verbal reports and her monitoring system both confirmed that depressive/anxious behaviors were being reduced. She still made no mention of the upcoming divorce.

During the next session, the eighth, the worker asked for and received permission to attend the divorce hearing the next week. The client still did not wish to discuss matters concerning the divorce during the counseling session. During the divorce hearing, she was not overwhelmed by the anxiety or pressure. Several times she asked her attorney or the judge for points of clarification. Immediately following the divorce, counseling sessions continued to focus on running. This treatment focus was at the client's insistence.

During the twelfth weekly session, she reported having no depressive-anxious episodes during the week. In addition, she had started a new job and felt "happy and fulfilled for the first time in a long time." An additional pleasant benefit for her during the course of treatment had been the loss of eighteen pounds. At this point, monthly appointments were arranged.

A six-month follow-up of the client's progress revealed that she was doing well at her new job and that she was continuing to lose weight. She had also resumed dating and felt that her contacts with the agency had been successful.

In both cases cited here, running was the major form of intervention. Nevertheless, even in this situation, a positive relationship often develops between the client and the therapist, and this may have been a factor in the successes experienced by the two clients described. In other instances, as previously noted, the authors have used running as one component in a traditional strategy of social work interventions.

Conclusions

Although the research indicates that running has positive psychosocial effects and may be useful as a part of the treatment of a variety of psychosocial problems, it must be recognized that much of this research is anecdotal. This is also true of the authors' experiences and is reflected in the case examples included in this article. More research is needed to answer a myriad of questions about the effects of running and its utility as a new form of therapy or as an aid to psychotherapeutic intervention:

1. Are psychological changes attributed to running the result of physiological and biochemical changes induced by prolonged exercise?

2. Are the psychological changes the result of the individual's improved self-esteem, which may come from a sense of physical fitness and mastery over a difficult challenge?

3. Are the psychological changes the result of the client's contact with an enthusiastic therapist who believes in running?

4. Will positive psychological changes brought about by running endure over a period of years?

Although research aimed at answering these and other questions is needed, the available evidence suggests that running has beneficial effects for some clients. In particular, running is potentially helpful to clients who have difficulty verbalizing, to those who exhibit symptoms of anxiety or depression, and to those with low self-esteem. Furthermore, running seems to hold promise as a cost-effective approach to psychosocial intervention because it provides symptom relief in a relatively short time and because clients can continue this activity on their own after termination with the therapist. Running also has positive physical side-effects that make it worthwhile to the client in fitness and an overall sense of well-being.

Running, like any other interventive approach, should not be regarded as a panacea. Some clients do not want to run or experience no positive psychosocial benefits from running, either by itself or in conjunction with other forms of intervention. Their particular problems may be atypical or unresponsive to running as a treatment. However, for other clients, a combination of running and other forms of psychosocial intervention may prove to be an optimal treatment plan. In addition, running may prove to be a viable alternative to medication for some clients. The use of running as an intervention in social work practice is likely to receive greater attention in the future, especially by those persons who are seeking out new and cost-effective ways to help their clients.

Notes and References

1. Valerie Andrews, *The Psychic Power of Running* (New York: Ballantine Books, 1978), p. 1.

2. Robert Andersen, "Running: A Road to Mental Health," *Runners World*, 14 (July 1979), p. 49.

3. For an overview of this research, *see* James F. Fixx, *The Complete Book of Running* (New York: Random House, 1977), pp. 13–35.

4. *See*, for example, Thaddeus Kostrabula, *The Joy of Running* (Philadelphia: J. B. Lippincott Co., 1976); and John H. Greist et al., "Antidepressant Running," *Psychiatric Annals*, 9 (March 1979), pp. 23–33.

5. Fixx, op. cit., pp. 6–8.

6. Fred W. Kasch, "The Effects of Exercise on the Aging Process," *The Physician and Sportsmedicine*, 4 (June 1976), pp. 64–68.

7. A. H. Ismail and L. E. Trachtman, "Jogging the Imagination," *Psychology Today*, 6 (March 1973), pp. 79–82.

8. Arnold Orwin, "The Running Treatment: A Preliminary Communication on a New Use for an Old Therapy (Physical Activity) in the Agoraphobic Syndrome," *British Journal of Psychiatry*, 122 (February 1973), p. 179.

9. Kostrabula, op. cit., pp. 129–130.

10. Myna M. Weissman, Jerome K. Myers, and Pamela S. Harding, "Psychiatric Disorders in a U.S. Urban Community: 1975–76," *American Journal of Psychiatry*, 135 (April 1978), pp. 459–462.

11. Robert S. Brown, Donald Ramirez, and John M. Taub, "The Prescription of Exercise for Depression," *The Physician and Sportsmedicine*, 4 (December 1978), p. 35.

12. Ferris N. Pitts, Jr., "The Biochemistry of Anxiety," *Scientific American*, 220 (February 1969), pp. 69–75.

13. Robert M. Post and Frederick K. Goodwin, "Simulated Behavior States: An Approach to Specificity in Physiological Research," *Biological Psychiatry*, 7 (December 1973), pp. 237–254.

14. Carlyle H. Folkins, Steve Lynch, and M. Melvin Gardner, "Psychological Fitness as a Function of Physical Fitness," *Archives of Physical Medical Rehabilitation*, 53 (November 1972), pp. 503–508.

15. Brown, Ramirez, and Taub, op. cit., pp. 35–45.

16. Greist et al., op. cit., pp. 22–33.

17. John B. Murphy, Robert N. Bennett, and James M. Hagen, "Some Suggestive Data Regarding the Relationship of Physical Fitness to Emotional Difficulties," *Newsletter of Research Psychology*, 14 (August 1972), pp. 15–17.

18. Richard R. Powell, "Psychological Effects of Exercise upon Institutionalized Geriatric Mental Patients," *Journal of Gerontology*, 20 (March 1974), pp. 157–161.

19. William P. Morgan, "Anxiety Reduction Following Acute Physical Activity," *Psychiatric Annals*, 9 (March 1979), pp. 36–45.

20. Ibid., p. 41.

21. William P. Morgan and D. H. Horstman, "Anxiety Reduction Following Acute Physical Activity," *Medicine and Science in Sports*, 8 (Spring 1976), p. 62.

22. *See* Fixx, op. cit., p. 17.

23. John H. Greist et al., "Running Out of Depression," *The Physician and Sportsmedicine*, 12 (December 1978), pp. 51–52.

24. Andersen, op. cit., p. 50.

25. Michael S. Bahrke and William P. Morgan, "Anxiety Reduction Following Exercise and Meditation," *Cognitive Therapy and Research*, 2 (December 1978), pp. 323–334.

26. Andersen, op. cit., pp. 49–50.

27. Kostrabula, op. cit., pp. 140–144; and William Glasser, *Positive Addiction* (New York: Harper & Row, 1976).

28. Brown, Ramirez, and Taub, op. cit., p. 45.

29. Kostrabula, op. cit., pp. 113–116.

30. Greist et al., "Antidepressant Running," p. 29.

31. For a good introduction to running, *see* James F. Fixx, op. cit.; and Hal Higdon, *Beginner's Running Guide*, Joan Ullyot, *Women's Running*, and Editors of Runner's World, *The Complete Woman Runner* (Mountain View, Calif.: World Publications, 1978, 1976, and 1978, respectively).

11

Family Support Systems and Unmarried Teenage Mothers

Joye S. Pursell and
Jane H. Pfouts

When schoolgirls become unmarried mothers, the problems they face and the solutions they find inevitably involve their parents, their sibs, and other family members. Yet all too often, practitioners fail to recognize and deal with the impact this crisis has on the total family system and with the effect the attitudes and behaviors of family members have on the future of the young mother and her baby. Family support is important during pregnancy and becomes even more crucial following the birth of the baby when patterns of interaction with kin have far-reaching consequences for the teenager and the child that she bears.

This article examines the effect of the family system on young unmarried mothers and their infants, drawing on evidence from the literature and from a study of ninety-six unmarried mothers, ages 12 to 16, in the year following delivery. The study's hypothesis is that families, far more than professionals, determine the success or failure of young unmarried mothers in completing the developmental tasks of adolescence and acquiring mothering skills that will enable the infants to begin their developmental tasks appropriately. Therefore, the authors believe that the kin network is by far the best resource that health and welfare practitioners have in helping young unmarried mothers and that additional professional efforts should be directed toward improving the functioning of the family units in which the young mothers live.

The Problem

Adolescent childbearing rates in the United States are among the highest in the world. Roughly 10 percent of the country's adolescents become pregnant, and 6 percent give birth each year.[1] According to data from the Alan Guttmacher Institute, roughly one-third of all adolescent births are conceived in marriage, one-third are conceived before a marriage takes place, and one-third are out of wedlock.[2] Pregnancy among 10 through 15 year olds presents the most disturbing problems. Because these young girls are still physically immature, the rates of medical complications for both the mother and the infant are high. Concomitantly, social problems increase dramatically for these young mothers.[3] According to Sarrel,

> the outlook for a stable family life is bleak. . . . The marital dissolution rate among teenagers who marry before the age of 18 is 80 percent within 5 years. . . . When girls keep their babies but do not marry, they often become trapped in a self-destructive cycle consisting of failure to establish a stable family life and repeat pregnancies.[4]

Although there is clear evidence that unmarried teenagers are sexually active in all races and social classes, the availability of alternatives to out-of-wedlock parenthood among sexually active adolescents varies by race and class.[5] Not surprisingly, black adolescents living in poverty are overrepresented among young unmarried parents because they and their families historically have been denied equal educational, medical, and economic resources to terminate the process through contraception, abortion, or youthful marriages subsidized by parents.[6] In addition, although black families, like other families in this culture, condemn out-of-wedlock pregnancy, they believe that babies should not suffer for their parents' mistakes and that the real sin would be to give away one's kin.[7] Therefore, the cultural expectation is that a young unmarried mother and her baby should be cared for at home by family members.[8] However, although black unmarried mothers continue to keep their babies to a greater extent than white unmarried mothers, this option is being taken by white women of all social classes far more often today than in earlier years.[9] Some young mothers of both races choose to marry; some live apart from the family in non-kin arrangements. Most, however, because of their immaturity and lack of resources, stay, at least temporarily or from time to time depending on circumstances, with their families of origin, and parental responsibility is shared by the kin group.

The increasing youth of unmarried mothers and the increasing desire of these girls not to give up their babies suggest that they and their children are likely to remain in semidependent situations in their kin groups more frequently and for longer periods of time than in the past. For this reason, it is important for practitioners and researchers to learn more about the dynamics of families that are blended in this way.

Kin Involvement

Because young unmarried adolescent mothers have made an unscheduled departure from the socially prescribed sequence of the life cycle, they are all subject to the stress and ambiguity inherent in an accelerated role transition.[10] Teenage mothers living with relatives are likely to find it particularly difficult to give up established patterns of dependency on adult kin, particularly their mothers, and to find a workable compromise between carrying out uncompleted adolescent developmental tasks and assuming the maternal role.

Teenage motherhood also imposes changes on the family system. Family roles, norms, and interactional patterns must adjust to the newly acquired adult status of the young mother and, at the same time, support her age-appropriate dependency and facilitate her efforts to complete adolescent developmental tasks. The most important link is likely to be between the young mother and her mother, and the nature of this relationship may well be a key factor in the success or failure of the family's adaptation to the new situation.[11] It may be, however, that the girl's father, a sib, a grandmother, or even someone outside the household is equally or more important than the girl's mother in helping or hindering the young mother's performance.

An important and difficult role demanded of the family system is to create a milieu that will make it possible for the girl to master the tasks of adolescence delineated by Erikson while still giving the necessary time and attention to her baby.[12] A major task of adolescence is the attainment of separation from one's parents. This process, which is difficult for most adolescents, is particularly problematic for young unmarried mothers who are in a situation that demands extensive emotional and material support from kin during the very period when, under other circumstances they would be moving toward autonomy.

Another major task of adolescence is the development of sexual identity and the ability to form lasting heterosexual relationships. Although pregnancy may serve as a means of solidifying sexual identification for some young unmarried girls, for others the traumatic aspects of out-of-wedlock motherhood exacerbate sexual issues and in-hibit the ability to move into lasting and satisfying love relationships.

A third important task of adolescence is the choice of a vocation and a commitment to work. Unscheduled early motherhood too often in-volves the loss of the educational and vocational experiences that would help adolescents prepare for adult roles.[13] According to Campbell,

> The girl who has an illegitimate child at the age of\16 already has 90 percent of her life script written for her. She will probably drop out of school, even if someone else in her family helps to take care of the baby. She will probably not be able to find a steady job that pays enough to provide for her and her child. . . . Her life choices are few and most of them are bad.[14]

Young teenage mothers do not want the bleak future that Campbell predicts; nor do their families want it for them. To create a better life for the girl, the family must actively help her achieve age-appropriate psychological and economic independence, to understand and handle her sexuality wisely, and to complete her education. However, in far too many cases, even with the best of intentions, the young mother and her family fail to normalize her life if social agencies and practitioners do not support their efforts.

Multiple Mothering

The second important function of families of adolescent mothers is sharing child rearing. The possibly deleterious outcome of multiple caretakers on the bonding of mother and child has received consider-able attention since Bowlby described the effects of maternal depriva-tion on children.[15] At present, even the most conservative opinion seems to be that it is not the amount but the quality of the mother-child interaction that determines whether the child will become attached. Studies of parenting in American black kin groups, in the Israeli Kibbutz, and in other cross-cultural situations suggest that multiple mothering may be a highly adaptive arrangement for both the imma-ture mother and her child.[16] Ainsworth believes that four interrelated factors determine the success or failure of multiple mothering: (1) the quality of the substitute care, (2) its consistency, (3) the developmental level of the child, and (4) the personality of the mother.[17]

Ideally, a multiple mothering arrangement enables the adolescent to proceed with her own developmental tasks while at the same time learning mothering skills from experienced adult role models. The baby may fare better in its young mother's kin group than in the exclusive care of one or even two immature and inexperienced teenaged parents. Young mothers have been described as irritable and impatient and as often torn between their own developmental needs and desires and those of their infants.[18] DeLissovoy found the teenage parents in his study "to be, with a few notable exceptions, an intolerant group, impatient, insensitive, irritable, and prone to use physical punishment with their children."[19] Because they were not familiar with developmental norms, DeLissovoy's sample had unrealistic expectations for their children and low tolerance for misdeeds such as crying. DeLissovoy also found that although the parents of the young couples were helpful in many ways, they also stressed early toilet training, strict discipline, and letting the baby "cry it out."

Health and welfare practitioners can help families develop successful patterns of multiple mothering by giving them information about sound child care principles and by assisting them in sorting out their family roles. The research suggests that the danger lies not in the domestic arrangement of multiple mothering, but rather in adult-child relationships that are insufficient, disturbed, or discontinuous. In some cases, the teenage mother, because of unwillingness or insecurity, turns over all child care responsibilities to others in the family.[20] In others, the pattern of teenage pregnancy is tacitly supported by the adolescent's mother, who is reluctant to give up her maternal role.[21] In still others, conflict over possession of the baby can disturb the child-parent relationship.[22] Most dangerous for the baby is the situation in which it is a pawn in a hostile-dependent relationship between mother and daughter.[23]

Clearly, multiple mothering is a family affair. It demands a family-focused approach by involved professionals both before and after the baby is born to help insure a successful outcome for both the adolescent mother and her child.

Study Sample and Design

The demographic characteristics of the study's ninety-six subjects are enumerated in Table 1. This small sample is strikingly similar in composition to Furstenberg's much larger group of unmarried mothers in that the subjects were mainly poor and black and tended to come from large one-parent families.[24] Family income was more likely to derive from Aid to Families with Dependent Children or other benefits than from wages, and socioeconomic status was almost exclusively lower or lower-middle class. In almost half the families, the study's subjects lived in large sibhoods with between four and nine other brothers and

TABLE 1.

CHARACTERISTICS OF THE TEENAGE UNMARRIED MOTHERS AT THE TIME
OF PREGNANCY ($N = 96$)

Age at the time of pregnancy		
Age 16	=	38
Age 15	=	32
Age 14	=	18
Age 13	=	6
Age 12	=	1
Unknown	=	1

Race

Black = 90
White = 6

History of pregnancy

One previous pregnancy terminated by abortion	=	7
No previous pregnancies	=	88
Unknown	=	1

Place of residence at time of pregnancy

Living at home with both parents	=	30
Living with mother	=	55
Living with father	=	2
Living with other relatives	=	8
Unknown	=	1

Number of children living in home including teenager and sibs

Teenager only child	=	8
Teenager plus one sib	=	11
Teenager plus two sibs	=	15
Teenager plus three sibs	=	16
Teenager plus four sibs	=	10
Teenager plus five sibs	=	15
Teenager plus six sibs	=	8
Teenager plus seven or more sibs	=	10
Unknown	=	3
Average number of children in family	=	4.5

Offspring of siblings living in home

Three offsprings of siblings	=	1
Two offsprings of siblings	=	4
One offspring of siblings	=	8
No offspring of siblings	=	80
Unknown	=	3

Source of household income

Primary wages		
father only wage earner	=	9
mother only wage earner	=	16
both parents employed	=	2
Primary benefits		
Aid to Families with Dependent Children	=	31
Social security	=	9
Combination of benefits	=	29

sisters, and in about 15 percent of the cases, one or more siblings were raising babies of their own in the home.

Roughly three-fourths of the sample were 15 or 16 years old, and one-fourth were 12 through 14. This was the first pregnancy for all but seven members of the group, each of whom had previously had an abortion. The nature of the sample reinforces the point made in the literature that although sexual activity among adolescents cuts across all social classes and races, viable alternatives to unplanned pregnancy and unmarried motherhood do not.

The authors' retrospective study of ninety-six young unmarried mothers tests the hypothesis that strong kin support significantly improves the life chances of both mother and child. The study is based on social, psychological, and medical data collected by the medical social worker, who worked directly with each of the ninety-six sample members between January 1974 and January 1979. At least two interviews were conducted by the medical social worker with each subject during prenatal visits to the Duke University Medical Center Adolescent Obstetrical Clinic, and following delivery, a minimum of two follow-up interviews were held by the same social worker in the Young Mother's Clinic of the Duke Pediatrics Department. The sample was restricted to those girls, 16 or younger, for whom this was the first pregnancy carried to term and who chose to keep their babies. Eliminated from the sample were pregnant teenagers seen at Duke during the time covered by the study who opted for abortion, marriage, or adoption rather than unmarried motherhood. The data collection and analysis emphasized the specific ways in which the presence or absence of support by kin affected the adaptation of the unmarried teenagers to pregnancy and to motherhood. Significant chi-square differences between girls who received strong material and emotional support from kin and those who did not were fitted to a causal model of outcomes during the first year of the baby's life.

Reactions to the Pregnancy

Table 2 presents the reactions of the teenagers and their families to the pregnancy. The initial reaction of the young subjects to their pregnancies was varied. Negative feelings predominated among 80 percent of the sample, which agrees with Furstenberg's study in which only one in five of his subjects expressed happiness about being pregnant.[25] Some of the girls in the sample were shocked and surprised. The reaction "I didn't believe it could happen to me" is indicative of the defense mechanism of magical thinking used by many young teenagers. Others reported a fear of parental reaction that was tantamount to an expectation of annihilation. Still others described feelings of sadness and depression accompanied by periods of crying. In some instances, indifference was expressed, which usually indicated to the hospital staff either an inability to express feelings or a defensive facade covering much stronger reactions. Only 20 percent of the sample expressed happiness about their pregnancies. However, since the information was collected a month or two after the discovery of the pregnancy, it is difficult to know how much the recollections were affected by intervening events.

Probably because of the stigma in this particular socioeconomic group against "giving away your flesh and blood," only three girls considered placing their babies, and none of them did so. As time passed and the crisis atmosphere created by the discovery of pregnancy receded, more positive feelings emerged among the sample. As new mothers, 57 percent were judged by hospital staff to be predominantly positive, 38 percent to be ambivalent, and only 5 percent to be predominantly negative toward their babies.

Data on the initial reactions of the fathers to the fact of pregnancy was obtained from the girls in only 57 percent of the cases. However, of the fifty-four men whose reactions were discussed by the young expectant mothers, three-fourths were said to be happy and pleased by their prospective fatherhood. This is in marked contrast to the negative reaction of the pregnant girls, for whom continuing responsibility for a child was a more sobering reality. During the first year of the baby's life, 41 percent of the fathers did provide some emotional support for the baby, but these were not necessarily the same fathers who were happy about the pregnancy.

Like the girls in the LaBarre study, the subjects in the study were neither promiscuous or prostitutes.[26] Most of them considered themselves to be "in love" and had had a relatively long relationship with the baby's father. Although almost half the men involved disassociated themselves from the pregnancy, many were supportive. Some prospective fathers engaged in such activities as accompanying the girls to clinic and prenatal activities, staying with them in labor and delivery, learning to care for the baby during the hospital stay, and continuing a regular relationship with the baby. In many cases, the mother and father "broke up" after delivery even though the father sometimes continued to see the baby and to contribute as best he could to its support. The youthfulness of these parents makes understandable their failure to sustain lengthy intense relationships with one another in a difficult situation and the inability of most of the fathers to assume more than limited economic responsibility for their children.

When asked about the initial responses of their families, most of the sample either professed not to know or characterized family reactions as angry, indifferent, or impassive. In only six cases was the reported response of parents and the kin one of pleasure at the prospect of a baby.

TABLE 2.

IMMEDIATE AND LONG-TERM RESPONSES TO THE PREGNANCY BY THE
TEENAGERS, THEIR FAMILIES, AND THE UNMARRIED FATHERS (N = 96)

Teenager's initial response to pregnancy		Unmarried father's long-term reaction to pregnancy according to teenager	
Depression	= 23	Both emotional and material support	= 41
Shocked surprise	= 13	Neither emotional nor material	
Fear of parental		support	= 38
reaction	= 9	Material support only	= 4
Fatalistic acceptance	= 17	Emotional support only	= 1
Ambivalence	= 14	Unknown	= 12
Happiness	= 20		
		Family's initial reaction to pregnancy according to teenager	
Teenager's long-term response to pregnancy			
		Anger	= 36
Positive	= 54	Shocked surprise	= 2
Ambivalent	= 37	Fatalistic acceptance	= 8
Negative	= 5	Indifference	= 11
		Happiness	= 6
Unmarried father's initial reaction to pregnancy according to teenager		Unknown	= 33
		Family's long-term reaction to pregnancy according to teenager	
Happiness	= 41		
Shocked surprise	= 3	Strong emotional and material support	= 50
Anger	= 1	Minimal emotional and material	
Indifference	= 5	support	= 39
Not told	= 4	Material support only	= 1
Unknown	= 42	Emotional support only	= 6

Among parents interviewed by the social worker, the majority admitted that they were angry or hurt at first, but said they the also felt that "anyone can make one mistake." With this attitude, 53 percent of the families eventually accepted the pregnancy and gave a great deal of support to their daughters both before and after delivery. Help from the remaining families continued to be more grudging and less satisfactory.

Both positive and negative adjustments on the part of family members to adolescent pregnancy have been noted in the literature. In LaBarre's sample, most families experienced a week or two of acute feelings of shock, grief, or consternation. Then, as parents often expressed it, "we realized we had to accept it and do the best we could."[27] Singer emphasized more negative family reactions, commenting that many families resented the girl and her pregnancy for its social dis-

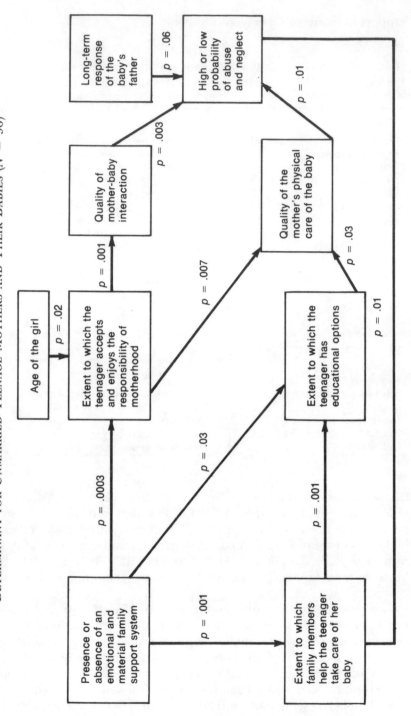

FIG. 1. CAUSAL CHART BASED ON CHI-SQUARE TESTS INDICATING THAT THE FAMILY SUPPORT SYSTEM IS A CRUCIAL DETERMINANT FOR UNMARRIED TEENAGE MOTHERS AND THEIR BABIES ($N = 96$)

grace and the extra economic hardships that another child entailed. Singer also found a significant relationship between the girl's health and comfort during her pregnancy and the degree of acceptance and emotional support provided by her mother.[28]

In the authors' sample, the nonsupportive kin groups were typically large families headed by females. It was in these families that mothers were least likely to come to the clinic to see the social worker or to take any interest in their daughter's obstetrical care or plans for the baby. The few who did talk with the social worker expressed hostility toward their daughters and saw the pregnancy and the expected baby as an imposition. The staff generally viewed nonsupportive family members as already overburdened with responsibility and therefore under-standably reluctant to assume an additional burden. Nevertheless, most of these families, as well as the more supportive families, allowed the teenagers and their babies to live at home following delivery. Eighty seven percent of the young mothers returned to their families, and only 13 percent went to live with other relatives, the baby's father, or friends.

Results

To test the hypothesis that family support is a crucial factor in the success or failure of young unmarried mothers, the authors first used the chi-square test to analyze relationships among the outcome vari-ables listed in Table 3. Significant results of the analysis were then fitted together in a hypothetical causal chart (see Figure 1). Although correlation does not prove causation, a causal chart is a useful heuristic device to make theoretical sense of empirical findings that are in accord with the hypothesized model. In the causal chart, it is the presence or absence of family support that triggers a statistically significant chain of behavioral outcomes for both the young subjects and their babies.

According to the data, it can be argued, as the model does, that family support directly affects the extent to which family members help the teenager take care of her baby ($\chi^2 = 4.64, p = 0.03$). The teenager's acceptance of the mothering role, in turn, affects both the quality of mother-baby interactions ($\chi^2 = 56.8, p = 0.001$) and the quality of the physical care she gives her baby ($\chi^2 = 19.1, p = 0.001$). Physical care of the baby is also linked to the educational options of the young mother ($\chi^2 = 6.51, p = 0.03$) in that babies of schoolgirls are better cared for than are babies of full-time mothers.

For the girls in the sample, it was family support that made the

TABLE 3.

ADJUSTMENT OF THE TEENAGERS AND THEIR BABIES IN THE YEAR
FOLLOWING DELIVERY ($N = 96$)

Agreement of teenager's plans for the future of the baby during pregnancy and after delivery		Quality of mother-baby interaction as judged by social worker	

Agreement of teenager's plans		Quality of mother-baby interaction	
Planned to keep baby during pregnancy and kept baby following delivery	= 93	Good interaction	= 51
		Questionable	= 35
Considered adoption during pregnancy but decided to keep baby following delivery	= 3	Hostile or rejecting	= 8
		Unknown	= 2

Teenager's living arrangements after delivery

At home with parent(s)	= 84
Living with relatives	= 9
Alone with baby	= 1
Living with baby's father	= 1
Living with a friend	= 1

Physical care of the baby as judged by hospital staff

Excellent	= 25
Adequate	= 58
Poor	= 13

Teenager's occupation after delivery

Goes to school	= 62
Full-time mother	= 29
Works part time	= 3
"Lives on the streets"	= 1
Unknown	= 1

Teenager's use of medical care for her baby as judged by type and number of clinic visits

Good—kept all clinic appointments	= 56
Adequate—kept most clinic appointments	= 27
Poor—kept few clinic appointments or had frequent trips to the emergency room	= 5
Unknown	= 8

Person providing primary care for the baby

Teenage mother	= 94
Maternal grandmother	= 2

Teenagers referred to protective services for abuse or neglect

No abuse or neglect referrals	= 83
Referred for child neglect	= 12
Referred for child abuse	= 1

Person providing supplementary care for the baby

Maternal grandmother	= 52
Paternal grandmother	= 4
Great grandmother	= 2
Sister(s)	= 11
Aunt(s)	= 4
No supplementary care (Mother has total responsibility)	= 17
Paid caretaker	= 6

difference between the girls who were able to cope with motherhood during the year following delivery and those who were not. Subjects in the sample who lacked adequate material and emotional support from kin were more likely to resent the responsibilities of the parental role, to have an indifferent or hostile relationship with their babies, to have little help in child care, and to drop out of school.

The younger the girl, the less likely she was to enjoy motherhood (χ^2 = 7.16, p = 0.02), and therefore the greater was her need for strong family support. The greater the number of siblings living in the home, the less closely bonded were the young mother and her baby (χ^2 = 9.05, p = 0.05), perhaps because there were too many potential parent figures for the baby to choose among. Neither socioeconomic status nor the source of family income were related to any outcome variables. Nor did the initial responses to the pregnancy by the girl, her family, or the baby's father forecast what their long-term responses would be or how well they would cope after the baby was born. Surprisingly, girls performed as well in the mothering role when their babies had medical problems, such as prematurity or heart murmurs, or when their own mothers were employed as when these complications were not a factor.

In 98 percent of the cases the young mother was the primary caretaker, and in 54 percent of the families the maternal grandmother provided most or all the supplementary care. In families that were rated as supportive, the girl's mother was likely to be the supplementary caretaker. Care in nonsupportive families was provided by other female kin, a paid caretaker, or the girl alone.

A record was kept of each girl's use of clinic facilities for her baby's medical care, and a strong relationship was found (χ^2 = 6.76, p = 0.001) between the degree of involvement of the maternal grandmother and the use of the clinic. Girls without extensive and consistent child care backup were more likely to be rated as giving their babies poor physical care (χ^2 = 19.4, p = 0.08) and were also less likely to remain in school (χ^2 = 31.2, p = 0.001) than were girls whose child care arrangements made it possible to combine motherhood and education.

A chi-square comparison was made between the thirteen mothers in the sample who were reported for abuse and neglect and the twenty-five mothers who were judged by the clinic staff to be giving excellent physical care to their babies. No significant differences were found between the two groups of young mothers in age, number of sibs, employment status of the maternal grandmother, the family's socioeconomic status, the medical status of the baby, or the initial reaction of the girl, her family, or the baby's father. However, the abusing and neglecting mothers differed significantly from the highly adequate mothers in a number of important ways. Abusing and neglecting mothers were significantly more resentful and angry about the unplanned pregnancy (χ^2 = 13.2, p = 0.001) as were their families (χ^2 = 21.3, p = 0.001) and the fathers of their babies (χ^2 = 17.2, p = 0.06). Because they were in disfavor with kin and the baby's father and were barred from participating in normal teenage activities by the burden of an unwanted child, these reluctant mothers, who were still children themselves, simply could not cope with the adult responsibility of mothering. In the sample, abuse and neglect were most likely when the mother was the sole caretaker, less likely when a relative was the supplementary caretaker, and least likely when the maternal grandmother filled that role (χ^2 = 8.47, p = 0.01).

Discussion and Summary

This study has clear implications for professionals who work with young unmarried mothers. Because strong and continuing kin support is crucial to the welfare of both the teenager and her baby, active professional intervention at the level of the family system cannot be avoided.

In the study there was no indication that multiple mothering as a system of child care was inevitably detrimental. It appeared that, among the study's subjects, the usual arrangement in which the girl served as the primary mother figure and was assisted by the maternal grandmother was highly adaptive. However, in this less-than-ideal situation of shared responsibility, there is always the danger of conflict or competition concerning the mothering role as well as the possibility that the child-caring performance of one or both caretakers might be deficient. Such problems can usually be ameliorated through appropriate family-focused intervention.

Much more serious is the situation in which the teenager receives insufficient material and emotional support from a hostile or indifferent family. Successfully raising a baby without a great deal of help from kin is beyond the capacity of almost all young teenagers. In such nonnurturant situations, if the family support system cannot be strengthened through interventive efforts, a responsible professional response is to activate or create alternative support systems and to provide supplementary agency services.

The key figure in the teenage mother's life is likely to be her mother.

In working with pregnant adolescents, the interdisciplinary staff at Duke came to agree with Young that "the influence of the mothers pervaded every area of planning that the teenage daughters engaged in for themselves and their expected babies.[29] Even though the girls' mothers typically were not pleased with the pregnancy, they usually felt it was the duty of the family to keep the baby, and their wishes prevailed over the ambivalence of their daughters. These young girls were simply too dependent and too unsure of their feelings to assert a strong preference for any other arrangement.

When the decision was made that a teenager would keep her baby, the Duke medical and social work staff members used individual conferences and group meetings to prepare her for the realities of child-rearing. Acquainting these young girls with the developmental stages of infancy and with mothering techniques is important because most of them visualize the baby as a lovable doll who will meet their needs rather than a living child with imperious needs of its own who will sicken or die if these needs are not met. It cannot be assumed that the teenagers' mothers or other adult female kin will be able or willing to model sound child-rearing practices. In addition to teaching mothering skills, the staff consistently tried to encourage and assist the girls in continuing school and resuming a normal social life.

Juggling the triple roles of teenager, daughter, and mother is far from easy. A number of girls in the sample became caught up in bitter conflicts with their babies' fathers when the young mother wanted to return to her normal teenage activities and the father insisted she stay home with "his" baby.

A third of the subjects also reported significant conflict with their mothers over the division of the mothering tasks and over questions concerning a proper balance for the girl between mothering and self-development. According to Williams,

> While most mothers are somewhat insecure in the parenting role with their first child, the young mother is even more insecure. . . . There seems to be a tendency for the grandmother to take over in caring for the infant, making it more difficult for the mother to accept parental responsibility about which she may already be ambivalent. On the one hand, she loves her child and wants to care for it well, but at the same time she does not want to be completely cut off from friends who are caught up with teenage pursuits antagonistic to childrearing.[30]

Bennis contends that when the mother-daughter relationship is conflictual and ill defined, the greatest danger for the child lies in confusing who mother is.[31] In some cases, neither the mother nor the grandmother assumes a real commitment to the child; in others, the grandmother may assume complete care of the child and blame her daughter for not taking more responsibility.

In anticipation of this conflict, the Duke staff includes the question of primary mothering in prenatal discussions with teenage patients and their mothers. Some can deal with the issue prior to delivery, but for others it becomes germane only after the conflict has become a reality. For the thirty-three girls in the study for whom conflict over mothering became a problem, the best resolutions were achieved when the young mother was willing to bring her mother to the well-baby clinic for an open discussion of the problem with the social worker. Also, during these conferences and in all postpartum contacts, the entire staff is careful to relate to the young mother, rather than to her mother, as the primary caretaker and thus to give her a greater feeling of self-assurance in the role.

Of the thirty-eight girls in the sample who received minimal emotional and material support from their families, thirteen abused or neglected their babies, but twenty-five did not. The authors believe that the difference in outcome between these two groups can be explained by the support the twenty-five nonneglecting mothers received from such alternative systems as other kin, the baby's father or his family, the Duke Medical Center staff, or personnel from other health or welfare agencies.

Every social worker working with a young unmarried pregnant girl who plans to keep her baby should routinely make as serious a study of the support system in which the girl plans to live as if it were an adoptive placement. If the girl's family support system is clearly too weak or too unmotivated to provide adequate nurturance for her and her baby, alternative or supplementary support systems should be used.

Even when the girl's own family is highly motivated to help her, professional intervention is often useful to help family members translate good intentions into a workable day-to-day partnership with the young mother. Although it is true that the family support system creates problems for the unmarried teenager, it is even more true that within that system, when it works well, can be found her best solutions.

Notes and References

1. Patrick C. McKenry, Lydia H. Walters, and Carolyn Johnson, "Adolescent Pregnancy: A Review of the Literature," *The Family Coordinator*, 28 (January 1979), pp. 17–28.

2. Alan Guttmacher Institute, *Eleven Million Teenagers: What Can Be Done about the Epidemic of Adolescent Pregnancies in the United States?* (New York: Planned Parenthood Federation of America, 1976).

3. *See*, for example, Edward Kennedy, *S.2533*, 94th Cong., 1st sess., October 21, 1975; Margie Rose, *Durham Morning Herald*, January 3, 1979, p. 1B; Robert L. Burket, Lois B. Johnson, and Joseph L. Rauh, "The Reproductive Adolescent," *Pediatric Clinics of North America*, 20 (November 1973), pp. 1005–1020; and Philip M. Sarrel, "Teenage Pregnancy: Prevention and Treatment," in *Problem Pregnancy: A Counseling and Resources Manual*, (Chapel Hill, N.C.: University of North Carolinia, 1972), pp. 1–13.

4. Sarrel, op. cit., p. 2.

5. Clark E. Vincent, *Unmarried Mothers* (Glencoe, Ill.: Free Press, 1961); and Maurine LaBarre, "The Triple Crisis: Adolescence, Early Marriage and Parenthood, Part 1," in *The Double Jeopardy, The Triple Crisis—Illegitimacy Today* (New York: National Council on Illegitimacy, 1969), pp. 1–23.

6. William Ryan, *Blaming the Victim* (New York: Pantheon Books, 1971).

7. Maurine LaBarre, "Psychosocial Implications of Teenage Pregnancies." Paper presented at the Seventh Congress of the International Association of Child Psychiatry and Allied Professions, Jerusalem, August 1, 1970.

8. Carol B. Stack, *All Our Kin* (New York: Harper & Row, 1974).

9. For comparisons of the frequency with which white and black unmarried mothers keep their babies, *see* Frank F. Furstenberg, Jr., *Unplanned Parenthood: The Social Consequences of Teenage Pregnancy* (New York: Free Press, 1976); Charles Bowerman, Donald Irish, and Hallowell Pope, *Unwed Motherhood: Personal and Social Consequences* (Chapel Hill, N.C.: University of North Carolina Press, 1966); Prudence Rains, *Becoming an Unwed Mother: A Sociological Account* (Chicago: Aldine Publishing Co., 1971); and Joyce A. Ladner, *Tomorrow's Tomorrow: The Black Woman* (Garden City, New York: Doubleday & Co., 1971). On the increased tendency among white unmarried mothers to keep their babies, *see* Helen L. Friedman, "Why Are They Keeping Their Babies?" *Social Work*, 20 (July 1975), pp. 322–323.

10. Lloyd Bacon, "Early Motherhood, Accelerated Role Transition, and Social Pathologies," *Social Forces*, 52 (March 1974), pp. 333–341.

11. Helen C. Friedman, "The Mother-Daughter Relationship: Its Potential in Treatment of Young Unwed Mothers," *Social Casework*, 47 (October 1966), pp. 502–506.

12. Erik Erikson, *Identity and the Life Cycle*, "Psychology Monograph Issues" (New York: International Universities Press, 1959).

13. Furstenberg, op. cit.

14. Arthur A. Campbell, "The Role of Family Planning in the Reduction of Poverty," *Journal of Marriage and the Family* (May 30, 1968), pp. 236–245.

15. John Bowlby, *Maternal Care and Mental Health* (2d ed.; Geneva, Switzerland: World Health Organization, 1952).

16. *See* Stack, op. cit.; Furstenberg, op. cit.; Melford Spiro, *Children of the Kibbutz* (Cambridge, Mass.: Harvard University Press, 1958); and Margaret Mead, "A Cultural Anthropologist's Approach to Maternal Deprivation," in *Deprivation of Maternal Care: A Reassessment of its Effects* (Geneva, Switzerland: World Health Organization, 1962), pp. 45–62.

17. Mary D. S. Ainsworth, "The Development of Infant-Mother Attachment," in Bettye E. Caldwell and Henry N. Ricciuti, eds., *Review of Child Development Research* (Chicago: University of Chicago Press, 1973), pp. 1–94.

18. *See* Robert R. Sears, Eleanor E. Macoby, and Harry Levin, *Patterns of Childrearing* (Evanston, Ill.: Row, Peterson & Co., 1957); and Linda L. Jenstrom and Tannis M. Williams, "Improving Care for Infants of School-Age Parents," *Sharing* (special supplement) (December 1975).

19. Vladimir DeLissovoy, "Child Care by Adolescent Parents," *Children Today*, 2 (July–August 1973), pp. 22–25.

20. Rains, op. cit.; and Jenstrom and Williams, op. cit.

21. David Schulz, *Coming Up Black: Patterns of Ghetto Socialization* (Englewood Cliffs, N.J.: Prentice-Hall, 1969); and Stack, op. cit.

22. Lee Rainwater, *Behind Ghetto Walls* (Chicago: Aldine Publishing Co., 1970).

23. Friedman, "The Mother-Daughter Relationship."

24. Furstenberg, op. cit.

25. Ibid.

26. LaBarre, "Psychosocial Implications of Teenage Pregnancies."

27. Maurine LaBarre, "Emotional Crises of School-Age Girls during Pregnancy and Early Motherhood," in Jane Schwartz and Lawrence Schwartz, eds., *Vulnerable Infants* (New York: McGraw-Hill Book Co., 1977), pp. 30–47.

28. Ann Singer, "A Program for Young Mothers and Their Babies," *Social Casework*, 52 (November 1971), pp. 567–577.

29. Barbara Berkman, Helen Rehr, and Alma T. Young, "Parental Influence on Pregnant Adolescents," *Social Work*, 20 (September 1975), pp. 389–391.

30. Tannis M. Williams, "Childrearing Practices of Young Mothers: What We Know, How It Matters, Why It's So Little," *American Journal of Orthopsychiatry*, 44 (January 1974), p. 72.

31. Judith Bemis, Evelyn Diers, and Ruth Sharpe, "The Teen-Age Single Mother," *Child Welfare*, 55 (May 1976), pp. 309–318.

12

Priorities in Black Adoptive Services

Jacquelyn Hampton

The goal of placing Black children in the best possible adoptive homes has created major difficulties for social workers. These difficulties stem, in part, from differences in the definitions of what constitutes "best possible" for Black children and from agencies' lack of knowledge about how to provide appropriate adoptive services for Black children. This author believes that these problems can be solved if practitioners follow the priorities outlined in this article for placing Black children. The article also discusses the philosophy behind these priorities and the implications they have for adoptive practice.

The decision-making process used in finding appropriate adoptive homes for Black children should be anchored in a child-centered philosophy that takes into account the special needs of Black children. Such philosophy must dispel the myths surrounding Black adoptive patterns and guide agencies to abandon the White-oriented standards for selecting adoptive families that have prevailed until recently and to apply standards appropriate to the realities of Black family life.

Briefly stated, the process of finding the best possible homes for Black children should be carried out in accord with the following sequence of priorities: (1) the placement of Black children in Black homes, an objective that should be pursued in conjunction with an outreach program to locate potential adoptive homes in the Black community, (2) the provision of high-quality Black foster care, thus buying time for the outreach program to identify Black adoptive homes, and (3) the consideration of White families for adoption only after all strategies to locate Black adoptive and foster homes have been exhausted. Moreover, the selection of a White family for the adoption of a Black child should be conditioned on a thorough agency evaluation to determine whether the White family is ready to deal with the realities of adopting and successfully rearing a Black child.

Faced with the dilemma of placing Black children in adoptive homes or allowing them to grow up in the foster care system, many social workers find themselves on uncertain professional ground. Many issues create constant division and confusion regarding this topic:

• Will Black families adopt in sufficient numbers to allow for the intraracial placement of Black children?

• Should White families be approved as adoptive parents for Black children?

• Are institutions or foster home placements preferable to transracial placements for Black children?

• What alternatives other than adoption are there for the permanent placement of Black children?

Although few people are academically, experientially, or professionally prepared to argue the issues, almost everyone, including social work professionals, prospective adoptive parents, and academicians, seem to be more than ready to fuel the raging debate over the placement of Black children. Close examination reveals that many of the issues are rooted in the American version of institutional racism. As with most race-related questions, the evidence for conclusive answers will not come easily. In the interim, responses are sensitive, polarization is extreme, and confusion is high. The madness would be compounded if the social worker providing direct services were to allow the ongoing philosophical battles to hinder the delivery of urgently needed services for the waiting Black child.

The purpose of this article is to offer the direct service provider a format that will allow logical decision-making in developing and implementing a permanent placement plan for the Black child. The suggestions offered here are primarily based on insights derived from the practice experiences of the Black Adoption Program and Services of the Kansas Children's Service League.

Foundation for Decisions

With numerous diverse attitudes prevailing about the placement of Black children, front-line social workers cannot be expected to make rational and appropriate decisions without some guidance. Nor should they be expected to predict the effects of transracial placements until there is sufficient evidence to substantiate a judgment.

However, the 1980s will demand that the social worker committed to optimal placements for Black children possess information and understanding that will lead to a rational decision-making technique. The premise of the blueprint for decision-making provided in this article is that although a child-centered focus is essential in any child-placement decision, race becomes a complicating issue when a Black child is involved. Each child's case results in a set of most and least desirable options. The qualified social worker skillfully assigns priorities to the options available and follows up with appropriate casework services, exhausting each choice in the order of its rank. Although the first, second, or even third best of the placement plans for the child may not materialize, the social worker who completes definite steps toward the optimal situation will arrive at a placement decision that will withstand the scrutiny of supervisors, the profession, the Black community, and society in general. Such a procedure assures the families of the children and the children themselves, who may someday wish to explore the circumstances of their childhood, that the worker has provided the best possible situation for the child. The steps suggested here are as follows:

1. The child-centered philosophical base for the placement of Black children should be specifically tailored to Black needs.

2. The set of options developed for each case should include race as a variable for determining priority.

3. The option selected should provide the situation with lowest risk.

Determining whether these steps have been followed could serve as an evaluative tool in assessing placement decisions. These steps require further discussion.

Philosophical Base   The term "child-centered" is certainly not a new one. Social workers involved in child welfare services know and understand the term and, for the most part, accept it as the philosophical base for service decisions about all children. There is, however, enough data to justify including race in the child-centered approach and making it an important consideration in determining the best interest of the child.[1] Although not always the determining factor in how relationships develop or how people interact and grow in their environment, race is a variable that must be considered in the psychological growth of an individual. Unless the American social system is substantially modified during the next twenty years, most placement decisions that are made for Black children will be far less than adequate if race is not a consideration.

A prerequisite to making acceptable placement decisions for Black children is that the social worker be personally and professionally committed to the idea that the Black child's interest deserves to be valued as highly as any other client's. The uniqueness of each waiting child demands that each case receive individual treatment and that all identifiable variables, including race, be explored. This should be the case regardless of whether the child is White, Oriental, Native American, Hispanic, or Black. Recognizing race as an important variable demands that the professional have a special knowledge and understanding of the racial factors that will be major considerations in placing a child.

A child-centered philosophical base appropriate for Black placements requires that the social work professional convert this knowledge and understanding into a healthy respect for the Black race. This must include an acknowledgment that the Black child is a lifetime member of the Black race.

It is important for the social worker to determine the extent to which he or she may be a victim of myths about Black people and Black adoptive patterns. The backlog of healthy Black children awaiting placement and the small number of Black placements have cultivated the fallacy that Black people do not adopt. Agencies have failed to recognize that Black existence has depended on the ability of Black families to adopt children of their own race and to teach these children the skills necessary to survive in a racist society.

The myth that Black families do not want to adopt Black children is perpetuated by agency policies and practices that involve standards appropriate to White families and that thereby screen out potential Black clients. This has meant basing selection criteria on such factors as infertility, a nonworking wife, material possessions, and fees. The capacity to assume the responsibilities of parenthood has often been considered secondary to these criteria, which, regardless of any usefulness they may have in evaluations of White families, are decidedly inappropriate for Black families. The issue is how to engage Black families in larger numbers in agency adoptions, rather than whether Black families are willing to adopt.

In light of these circumstances, it would be helpful for the social worker committed to developing an appropriate philosophical base for Black placements to participate in some self-analysis. The following statements provide a focus for such an analysis.

- I believe that Black children deserve the best homes possible.
- I believe that my agency should take action in placing Black children in the best homes possible.
- I believe that Black people can and will adopt Black children since they have always adopted informally.
- I believe that traditional agency policies and practices have hindered the legal placement of Black children in Black adoptive homes.
- I believe that front-line social workers should affect agency policies and practices.
- I believe that Black people and other ethnic groups can love and care for children of their own race.
- I believe that Black children fit naturally into Black environments and that, in a reasonably normal situation, the Black home would offer the lowest psychological risk for a Black child.

The social worker who can affirm each of these statements has acquired the foundation of a child-centered philosophy that would serve the interests of a Black child. Such a philosophy can be translated into the following set of propositions:

> Black children deserve the best home possible. Black families can love and care for these children and provide the least psychological risk. Agency policies and the practices of agency staff should assure that these homes are found.

Many professionals will see this logical construct as too simplistic. They will argue that there are far too many extenuating circumstances to apply this simple logic consistently as a basis for placement decisions. They will allow their personal values on race relations to fog their thoughts on what is best for the Black child. Frustrations arising out of past failures to reach out to Black families will weigh on the minds of many professionals, as will guilt feelings about having made transracial placements or about not having placed a child in a certain home. If these rationalizations and doubts are intensified by the existence of a heavy caseload, by responsibility for many tasks beside placement, or by insensitive supervisory and administrative structures, the social worker may doubt the feasibility of incorporating this philosophical framework into his or her practice.

The dedicated social worker should not dwell on past actions if he or she feels capable of offering placement services to Black children. There is nothing to be gained from lamenting the untenable mistakes of the agency, the profession, or society. What is important is that the social worker who agrees with the philosophical base just set forth begin to shape practice decisions accordingly.

Developing and Analyzing Options   Determining the most appropriate action for each case is a result of considering all possible options and their probable long-range effects. This means that placements which involve the lowest risk for the child should be given highest priority. Because transracial adoptive placements have become numerous only during the last ten years, much of the research on those placements, such as *Mixed Families: Adopting across Racial Boundaries* by Ladner, acknowledges that more time is needed for the children to mature before the long-term effects of such adoptions can be evaluated.[2] However, studies of intraracial adoptions among Black families such as *Informal Adoption among Black Families* by Hill clearly document the positive effects of this form of adoption.[3] It is logical to conclude, therefore, that, for the present at least, intraracial placements are most desirable and that decisions to place transracially should occur only upon the depletion of intraracial resources. This logic is the basis of the set of priorities that follows:

Priority 1: Pursue intraracial placement through vigorous outreach to the Black community. This is the preferred course of action, and it is facilitated by the following procedures:

• Produce a current assessment of the child with a description of the child's physical features that uses verbal imagery and clear color photographs.

• Develop a recruitment design to attract Black adoptive applicants, perhaps borrowing ideas from successful recruitment programs elsewhere in the country, but always shaping any such program to the characteristics of the local community.

• Develop a local, state and national mailing list to register each child and, in the absence of a state or local exchange, send letters explaining the needs of each child directly to other agencies and include the child's current social history and a picture.

• If the foster parents are Black, assess the feasibility of the foster parents' adopting the child or retaining legal guardianship. The emphasis should be on acquiring subsidy payments and activating other support systems.

• Approach the extended family as a source for the adoption if this is possible and does not create further legal or family problems.

• Investigate the possibility that close friends of the family may be willing to act as legal guardians and surrogate parents to children, although the notion of a formal adoption procedure could seem too complicated, expensive, or even unnatural to them, as it might to extended family members as well.

• In the event of the failure of all these efforts at intraracial placement, assess the factors that could have had negative effects and consider the following questions: Did agency policies or practices interfere with the response of Black applicants? Were your efforts stifled by an insensitive administrative or supervisory hierarchy? Did your professional techniques turn off prospective applicants? If any of these situations undermined the outreach, a new recruitment effort should be initiated.

Priority 2: Insure the best possible services to the waiting child. Absorption with adoption as the primary placement goal without giving appropriate attention to the child's foster care placement could negate the viability of the very avenue that is most likely to ensure a permanent placement.

Although foster care should mean temporary placement, it is often the case that a child in this situation is in the best possible home, at least for the time being. The key to providing adoption services during the period of foster care has been clearly defined by such programs as the Oregon Project, a two-year demonstration effort aimed at overcoming barriers to permanent planning.[4] The Oregon Project makes it clear that when a child is in foster care, permanency should be the intent of placement services. This insures that a child's placement is never left to chance, but is determined by conscientious and methodical planning. This type of casework will give the social worker confidence not to settle on an adoptive placement that is only marginally desirable for the child.

At the Black Adoption Program and Services of the Kansas Children's Service League, the processes of child assessment, of recruitment and home assessment, and of matching the children with families have sometimes meant waits of over a year for older children and siblings. This is a long time, but the homes located by these careful procedures have low rates of turnover. The implication of this experience for the importance of high-quality foster care is evident, and this is true even for the program that vigorously reaches out to Black families. Social workers should not be tempted to make hasty decisions. A way of measuring the appropriateness of an action is to assess the elements on which that choice was based. Children should not drift in foster care, but an inappropriate, hastily arranged adoptive placement could be worse than unlimited foster care.

This observation is not meant to hinder the swelling surge of immediacy that now surrounds the quest for permanency through adoption. The purpose here is to emphasize the interrelatedness between high-quality foster care and high-quality adoption services. Most adoption workers know many cases in which inadequate foster care negatively affected the adoptive placement. Conversely, a successful relationship between the child and the adoptive family often owes much to the quality of the care given the child during the foster home placement.

Assessment of White Families

The two placement decisions with the highest priority are not the only options. The experience of the Black Adoption Program and Services and other adoption recruitment programs demonstrates that these two primary options are available in most cases and that they offer the lowest risk to the Black child, but other circumstances will find the social worker considering other options. Social workers are often pressured to consider transracial placement, since waiting White families may provide speedy placement resources. An agency tends to reward workers for numbers of placements when this measure of agency success has a direct effect on funding and possibly on the program's existence. The needs of the agency and the family are thus given precedence over the needs of the child.

As defined in this article, the child-centered placement philosophy for Black children permits a transracial placement to be considered only when (1) the outreach to the Black community has been exhausted, (2) enough time has been allowed for case planning and outreach to exhaust the possibility of finding a Black adoptive family, and (3) the evaluation of the casework practice substantiates that all intraracial options have been eliminated. Home-study processes of the Black Adoption Program and Services call for raising the following issues with White families that request to adopt a Black child:

• What is the family's motivation for adopting transracially? Caseworkers are advised to beware of those who wish to build race relations or who profess to see no difference in races of people. The adoption of Black children should not be used to experiment in race relations, to ease a guilty conscience, or to win adherents for a religious practice.

• Will the adoption of a Black child be accepted by relatives of the White family? A family that will be rejected by its extended family because of a transracial adoption will have many problems explaining this rejection to the child because it is likely to be accompanied by many other rejecting messages that will come from the White community and society.

• Will the child have numerous Black contacts and relationships? A good friend is not enough; the racial makeup of the community is important. The child should be able to grow in an environment that permits many Black relationships to be formed naturally. Is the family willing to consider relocation if necessary?

• What has been the extent of the family's exposure to the Black community? Do they have numerous relationships with Black people? A lack of such exposure and relationships is an indicator of the child's position as an experiment. This does not have to be intentional, but it is inevitable. Reading books about Black life and having a Black acquaintance cannot substitute for the kind of intimate relationships that can only be formed by living in the Black community or by having long-term relationships with diverse groups of Black people.

• Will the family accept the physical features of the Black child? It is not possible to guarantee the skin color or hair texture of a child under 5 years old. Accepting a child's features also means a commitment to learning to care for those features. The family should receive knowledge of how to care for Black features before a child is placed.

• Does the family have ample references from the Black community? The family should be referred by more than one Black person, and the persons referring the adoptive family should have experience in child rearing and an extended relationship with the family. Relatives and friends of the adoptive family should also recommend that the family receive a child.

The non-Black family that does not meet each criterion should be considered a higher risk than one that meets all of them. This assumption is based on the experience of the Black Adoption Program and Services, which uses these criteria regularly in selecting Black families for Black children. To ignore these or comparable procedures would compromise the standards of selecting an appropriate home for the Black child.

Policy Implications

Social work must play "catch-up" in providing permanent placement services to Black children. Demonstration efforts in recruiting Black homes and providing high-quality foster care services lead to the conclusion that the backlog of older, waiting Black children can be diminished. The issue is how to act on the alternatives in placement in a way that minimizes the risks for the Black child. Agency policies will affect, if not determine, the front-line social worker's choice of options. The following policy recommendations are given in hopes that the Black child's interest will be served over that of the agency:

1. Each case involving a waiting child should receive foster care services based on a permanency planning goal.

2. Each case involving a Black child should be assigned to a social worker and supervisor who have training in or close familiarity with the life-style of Black families, and they should know how adoptive recruitment and permanency planning apply to Black families.

3. Every attempt should be made to place the Black child with a Black family before a transracial placement is considered.

4. Priority should be given to the three preceding policy suggestions through providing adequate funds and professional incentives.

Prior to the 1960s, the common practice was to label the Black child "hard to place" and let foster care take its course. However, as healthy white infants became scarce and the number of White families requesting children increased, a trend toward the transracial placement of Black children emerged. Agencies claimed that Black families would not adopt, and they often found it more lucrative to place the child with a White family.

With the emergence of programs like the Black Adoption Program and Services, clear evidence began to accumulate that Black families are available to adopt Black children. Further, evidence emerged that agencies screen out potential Black applicants with criteria tailored to select White applicants.

The existence of Black family resources for Black children has been proved, but this still has not had the impact on permanent placements for Black children it should. The crucial factor could be the readiness of the front-line professional social worker. This article has acknowledged that sound social work practice in permanent placement planning requires a child-centered focus for every child. However, to omit race as a determining factor for Black children is contrary to the child-centered focus. Social work practice in the 1980s faces diverse challenges in serving Black children. Meeting the challenges will require an evaluation of agency policies and the formation of administrative and supervisory responses that will assure the selection and training of qualified staff. Until this is attended to, the Black child's interest will never be served with a child-centered focus. Foster care will continue to take its course.

Notes and References

1. Joseph Goldstein, Anna Freud, and Albert J. Solnit, *Beyond the Best Interest of the Child* (New York: Free Press, 1973), pp. 3–6.

2. Joyce A. Ladner, *Mixed Families: Adopting across Racial Boundaries* (Garden City, N.Y.: Doubleday & Co., 1977). *See also* Andrew Billingsley and Jeanne Giovannoni, "Research Perspectives on Interracial Adoptions," in Roger R. Miller, ed., *Race, Research, and Reason: Social Work Perspectives* (New York: National Association of Social Workers, 1969), pp. 57–77.

3. Robert B. Hill, *Informal Adoption among Black Families* (Washington, D.C.: National Urban League Research Department, 1977).

4. Victor Pike et al., *Permanent Planning for Children in Foster Care: A Handbook for Social Workers* (Portland, Oreg.: Regional Research Institute for Human Services and U.S. Department of Health, Education, & Welfare, 1977).

13

Differential Utilization of Social Work Manpower

Werner W. Boehm

The quest for clarity about the differences in the functions of social workers with bachelor of social work (BSW) and those with master of social work (MSW) degrees is among the most urgent tasks confronting the profession. Unfortunately, the profession is far from even approaching that task. In a critical review of the Baer and Federico study *Educating the Baccalaureate Social Worker*, this author suggested that empirical studies be used to determine whether there is a difference in function between MSW and BSW personnel.[1] Undoubtedly, other types of empirical studies might also be suggested. A common complaint among concerned social work practitioners and educators is that there is a dearth of empirical data.[2] Although empirical studies are urgently needed, there is an equally urgent but prior need for a conceptual framework of social work practice that brings together the several goals, objectives, functions, and intervention modes of social work. This conceptual task should precede the empirical undertaking to avoid the risk of studying elements that may be marginal rather than central to social work. Any empirical studies of social work manpower should be informed by and reflect a social work perspective.

Consequently, this article addresses two tasks: (1) it identifies the components of social work practice and casts them into a coherent framework, and (2) it relates these key functions to the current social work reality—the existence of MSW and BSW professionals—and establishes strategies for manpower that seem plausible in the light of

158

existing practice patterns and contemporary characteristics of American society. This is a large undertaking, and the present article can do no more than set the stage for a searching analysis and well-informed empirical steps.

The author, it must be noted, has no ideological reservation about the desirability of having two levels of professional social work personnel. However, the process followed in establishing these two categories was seriously flawed. The author, as a member of the national board of the National Association of Social Workers (NASW) in 1968 when the decision was made to establish the two categories, voted against the motion not out of opposition to the idea of a BSW, but because, in the absence of an identification of differential functions for each type of professional, such a decision seemed to have a strong potential for damaging the profession.

Framework of Practice

In the light of previous formulations of the scope of social work practice, including those by Bartlett, Studt, and the present author, it is convenient, first, to identify the populations that are served, actually and potentially, by social workers; second, to specify the broad purposes or policies social work seeks to achieve through practice; third, to enumerate the program categories that are in existence or that need to come into being; and, fourth, to identify the nature of the practice social workers engage in and any they might undertake in the future.[3] These four P's—population, purpose or policy, program, and practice—can be linked together by a fifth P, the perspective that is characteristic of social work and that tends to differentiate it from other human service professions.[4]

Perspective The perspective of social work—its philosophy or orientation—animates and holds together and envelops the various aspects of the profession. This perspective consists of the social work ideology, the values social workers embrace and try to practice. These values constitute the major element in what distinguishes social work from other human service professions. Although we social workers try to practice what we preach more than do other occupations, we cannot effectively rest our claim for distinctiveness on that alone.

As has been pointed out by Bartlett and others, social work's claim to an exclusive domain must also rest on the characteristic configuration of elements that compose professional social work practice.[5] Thus, the distinctive gestalt of social work emerges not in its concepts and context, but in how it uses concepts and how it links them to each other, to the value structure and sanctions of social work. This is what has led the social work profession to develop its unique concept of social functioning as defined later in this article.

Population   Typically and predominantly, the population groups that come to the attention of social workers are disadvantaged. They are individuals, families, and groups who have been damaged economically, socially, culturally, or personally. They may be struggling with deficiencies of economic or social resources. They may be beset by the inadequacies of existing social structures or handicapped by a mismatch between their needs and the opportunities to meet them. The population served by social work also includes individuals, families, and groups who have been handicapped or are underdeveloped or deprived in the realms of education or physical or mental health; or their degree of social growth, maturation, or socialization may be insufficient for their life tasks.

It is widely recognized that these groups constitute the bulk of the social work clientele, but there is, in addition, another category of persons who, although not afflicted in the same way or to the same degree, show the inexorable ravages of daily living that take the form of alienation, insecurity, incapacity or discomfort in interpersonal relationships, general malaise, unhappiness, and misery. This population, too, deserves the ministrations of the social worker. Their only and fortunate difference from the other groups serviced by social workers is that because they are not economically or socially deprived, they tend to focus on intangible deficits. Although the other categories of people who come to social work's attention show these deficits, these intangible deficiencies tend to be overlooked when basic ingredients of effective living are missing.

A profession that claims to carry out a societal mandate needs to serve all segments of the population. Different groups may at times require priorities in the allocation of funds and manpower and may even need preferential treatment, but the avowed stance of the profession should be that it is available to all members of society in ways appropriate to their different needs.

Purpose   The range of social work activities is so great and varied that it is desirable to bring them together in a formulation which identifies what these activities have in common and which also classifies the activities into categories. A number of formulations are available. They all derive from a common social work perspective, which, to quote Bartlett, is that "the unit of attention in social work practice is the interaction between the demands of the environment and the coping patterns of the individual."[6]

In earlier articles, this author suggested that the purposes of social work are essentially twofold—to bring about and assist in the processes of (1) social rehabilitation and social habilitation and (2) social reconstruction and social construction.[7]

The activities designed to achieve social rehabilitation are most familiar. This category includes the traditional work of caseworkers and group workers who help people restore their lost or reduced capacities for the performance of social roles in the family, neighborhood, and community. These clients need this support because the aptitudes they once had were overwhelmed by personal, social, or societal circumstances or events.

Social habilitation, by contrast, helps people acquire capacities that they have never possessed, but that are necessary to their living meaningful lives. Everyone needs to learn new roles and to modify traditional ones in the course of a lifetime, whether the changes are brought on by maturing and aging or occur as a result of political or economic upheavals or some natural disaster. In any case, losing habitual pathways and being forced into new and often unknown ones can be a frightening experience. Some are able to make these changes unaided, but many require the ministrations of a caring profession.

These clients may need support either because of deficiencies in societal resources or because of personal or social deficiencies. Much of the profession's work with deprived populations belongs here. Social workers not only help to restore social functioning, but also, whenever possible, assist the client in working toward self-actualization. Many members of society, regardless of their socioeconomic level or sociocultural membership, at some point or other in their lives become incapable, temporarily or permanently, of carrying out their usual life tasks.

Social reconstruction and social construction are purposes that have always been claimed by the profession, but only recently have they become part of its province in a systematic way. These purposes fall in the realm of social policy and planning and entail the careful analysis of existing social welfare programs to determine whether they achieve their stated goals. Hence, there needs to be assessment whether the programs contain the services they purport to contain and whether they reach the consumers for whom they are destined. Such analyses may lead to the redesign of programs or to changes in patterns of delivery and access. These endeavors fulfill the purpose of social reconstruction. By contrast, social construction seeks primarily to create new welfare policies to address unmet or insufficiently met social needs.

Both purposes of social work have a preventive cast.[8] Although social construction and social reconstruction are more likely to achieve primary prevention of social dysfunctioning, social habilitation and rehabilitation, especially the former, achieve not only tertiary but also secondary prevention—they deal with existing instances of dysfunctioning and also reduce their scope and strength.

Programs   Where are the purposes of social work carried out? What are the social and institutional contexts in which social work purposes and functions take place?

This question can be answered easily because it can be shown that social work is embedded in those social institutions which are concerned with social welfare either directly or indirectly. The programs that carry forward the purposes of social work are the personal social services, including services for children and the aged; income maintenance programs; health and mental health programs; housing and urban renewal programs; educational programs; and the judicial and correctional systems.

Social work is not, and it need not be, the only profession in most of these programs. The programs employ a great variety of social welfare personnel, who differ in skills, in knowledge, and in levels of training and education. What makes these programs pertinent to social work is that in each of them the key purposes of social work—social habilitation and rehabilitation and social construction and reconstruction—not only have a place, but they constitute the salient and often essential component.

Practice   In light of the foregoing, the old formulation that the kernel of social work activities consists of various types of intervention warrants reaffirmation.[9] The activities social workers engage in and the tasks they perform in conjunction with and on behalf of beneficiaries of social services cause them to enter into and intervene in other persons' lives.

What then is characteristic of the interventions? What makes them social work interventions? Their special social work character stems from a concept of social functioning that is unique to social work. First, in keeping with the formulations of Bartlett and Gordon, the unit of attention is the interplay of personal, social, and societal factors.[10] Second—and this is a departure from Bartlett and Gordon—social functioning is seen not as an independent, but as a dependent variable.[11] Individual functioning or dysfunctioning depends not on the interaction of the coping tasks and the environmental demands, but on personal, social, economic, communal, societal, political, cultural, and other factors. The social worker's task is to ascertain which of this vast array of factors need to be taken into consideration and assessed to determine the nature of the problem and to design strategies for intervention.

A view of social functioning as dependent on a host of personal social and societal factors permits the question, What is the nature of social work intervention? Can its many activities be classified and, if so, how? The activities of social work constitute a systematic approach to problem-solving and consist of four processes: (1) understanding and assessing the social situation, (2) designing strategies of intervention, (3) implementing the design, and (4) evaluating the results.

Understanding and assessment entails asking what persons, circumstances, situations, and conditions are involved; what the impact of the situation is on key persons and others in it; what personal, social, and societal resources are at play and which ones can be brought into play; and what coping patterns are operating, how effective they are, and which ones might be created, added, improved, or eliminated? Understanding and assessment entail inquiry and judgment, and the outcome is a formulation that specifies the nature of the problem—the factors associated with its occurrence, and the factors that are likely to contribute to its continuation, aggravation, elimination, or disappearance.

Completing an assessment makes possible the next step in the process, the design of a strategy of intervention. The social worker asks, What should be done? What factors need to be dealt with and changed? Which ones should be left alone? What additional forces can be mobilized? Which ones actually and potentially are in play and can be realigned? How or in what ways can significant others, consumers, services providers, influence groups, and others become meaningfully active in the process of change?

The processes of understanding, assessment, and design require the highest level of professional sophistication and competence. The other two processes, execution of the design and evaluation, are also essential. The execution of a design frequently requires joint activities involving consumers, significant others, providers, and professionals.

These efforts consist of the great variety of activities that go into rendering concrete services and modifying relationships.

Evaluation is less frequently implemented than is desirable. It consists of those activities professionals undertake to determine whether and to what extent the objectives established in designing the intervention have been accomplished. These processes of execution and evaluation require a lower level of competence than assessment and design, if they can be carried out under the tutelage of an experienced, knowledgeable practitioner.

Multitude of Roles Another component of the distinctiveness of social work, one that has not been generally recognized or acknowledged, is that social workers carry out a wide variety of activities in a complex and varied network of institutions. This permits the profession to establish social work roles not only in that component of society usually identified as social welfare, but also in the social welfare component of social institutions in which social work as a profession performs only a partial function. As Gurin said, "Social work has a different network of relationships, reference groups, and institutional responsibilities from that of other professions."[12]

Division of Labor

The model of manpower deployment that follows from the foregoing formulation of the framework of social work is that the tasks of assessment and design should be performed by the social work practitioner with a high level of education, namely, the MSW. BSWs can, and frequently do, carry out implementation of the design, including delivering services, discovering social and societal resources, making the resources available to consumers who need them, identifying the need for resources, and changing patterns of resource delivery.[13] The performance of the BSW should be monitored by an MSW, who thus takes overall responsibility for the intervention. This ensures that the most competent professional assumes responsibility for the intervention and at the same time allows for the use of BSWs. However, this structure is an ideal that realities of funding, distance, and organization often render unattainable.

The division of labor suggested here does not dispense with the participation in the intervention enterprise of other social welfare personnel, such as technicians, aides, and the like. What the model posits is that the MSW be viewed as the key practitioner and entrusted with the assessment and design of the intervention strategy, that the BSW be entrusted with the tasks of implementation and evaluation wherever possible, and that the overall undertaking be monitored by the MSW to whatever extent possible.[14]

Unfortunately, there is not enough descriptive literature available to warrant even a suggestion about the fourth element in the set of social work activities, namely, evaluation. If the design of the evaluative steps can be undertaken by an MSW, perhaps the execution can be entrusted to a BSW. If overall responsibility for all four processes is lodged with the MSW, this phase of the model should be able to be carried out by BSWs. In the absence of an MSW as the responsible professional, it would be difficult to envision a role for the BSW in the evaluation process.

How does this model jibe with the realities of current practice? At present, the model is in operation only in rare instances in some of the personal social service programs and in the health and mental health fields. However, many MSWs function as clinical practitioners in agencies in the private sector or as supervisors of clinical practitioners with additional responsibilities for difficult primary relationships. It is not inconceivable that even in the voluntary field the MSW supervisor will eventually find it appropriate to entrust service delivery to BSWs. As new patterns of coordinated service structures develop combining the delivery of concrete (hard) and relationship (soft) services, a division of labor between MSW and BSW workers such as the one outlined here will become a possibility. When this will be possible and the details of how it will occur will have to be made clear by empirical studies that focus on the personnel carrying out these and similar functions.

The model suggested here reflects the predominantly urban characteristics of social work, a high degree of population density, the availability of a great number of MSWs, and the consumer's close proximity to centers of practice. In rural areas and in the vast expanses of western states, the model would nevertheless be possible provided there is flexibility. For instance, MSWs could provide consultation through a modern process of circuit riding—expanding on the present uses of the telephone and closed circuit television. Such arrangements would not only overcome the dearth of MSW personnel in certain parts of the country and the handicaps of distance, it also would accommodate the tendency of agencies with limited budgets to employ BSWs in situations where they would prefer MSWs. Consultation, staff development, and continuing education programs provided by MSWs specially trained for such activities would enhance the MSW's overall responsibility for the intervention processes and improve the services provided by BSWs. The effectiveness of MSWs and BSWs in such roles should be validated through empirical studies, a step NASW should undertake or stimulate.

The approach suggested here leaves out the generalist role sometimes suggested for the BSW. The proponents of this role prescribe generalist responsibilities for the BSW and specialist functions for the MSW. The problem with the generalist role is that it has few empirical referents and is therefore vague and ill defined. Most important, the general practitioner may need preparation that goes beyond that of the specialist. Some have suggested that the MSW and the BSW both perform specialist services, with MSWs dealing with more complex situations. Such a division of labor in practice is difficult to conceptualize let alone to execute. Instead, both the BSW and the MSW should execute different functions. Each should have a realm of activity in the complex of service delivery, the MSW handling design, assessment, and monitoring as well as supervision and consultation, the BSW carrying out implementation and evaluation.

This raises the question about which arenas of service can have such a division of labor? At present the answer is that this can best be done in personal social services. In the personal social services that are the province of voluntary agencies, MSWs and BSWs are already deployed along these lines.[15] Although such deployment can theoretically be matched in the personal services provided by the public sector, it remains to be seen whether, even if funding were available, the reorganization and rearrangement of services in public agencies would lead to that kind of deployment. Although compatible with current patterns of funding, such a division of labor may be incompatible with current bureaucratic structures, and demonstration projects would have to test whether such deployment patterns are feasible for public operations.

Specialists are needed not only to staff personal social services, but also to manage them. Traditional social work limited itself to providing front-line services and supervision and consultation, but the profession has recently begun to train MSWs to manage and administer personal social services. Continued efforts in this direction may have positive consequences for the profession in all social institutions that contain a social welfare component, including health and mental health organizations, income maintenance programs, educational institutions, the judicial and correctional systems, and housing and urban renewal programs. A deliberate and explicit decision by the profession to take responsibility for the direction and management of social services in these institutions would provide employment opportunities for the MSW who is a specialist in management and administration and, more important, would provide those institutions with a social work perspective.

This discussion has so far been limited to delineating the functions of MSW and BSW specialists in direct social intervention—the provision of personal social services and the administration of direct services. However, the profession has also begun to engage in societal intervention in the social institutions just named. It has begun to equip personnel with special skills in social need identification, social resource coordination, social resource creation, social resource delivery, and social resource utilization.[16] These specialists possess functional skills that can be subsumed under the headings of planning, coordination, and social policy analysis and execution. They are specialists in design and evaluation, but may also function as managers and evaluators. Their activities are frequently in leadership roles and constitute social work practice. They are deployed in the personal social service complex and in the social welfare sections of other social institutions.

Although a few MSW programs are preparing personnel with these skills, there is no indication that the profession is committed to the creation of this kind of specialist. If it moves to this direction, experimentation in the restructuring of services and redesign of professional practice will be essential. It is unclear that a similar form of specialization can occur on the BSW level, but even if this is not practical, the emergence of a great variety of specialists on the MSW level poses an exciting venture for the profession.

Implications for Education

The consequences for educational policy and curriculum of developing such a broad range of practice specializations cannot be spelled out in this article, but three observations are in order. First, developing MSWs with different practice specializations will require that MSW programs offer a variety of parallel specializations, but these offerings should be organized in a way that gives all MSWs a common base of knowledge, attitudes, and skills. The content of such MSW programs needs to have more depth and breadth than most MSW programs now possess.

Second, the development of specialists on the BSW level also requires a revamping of the content of educational programs. Many BSW programs are foreshortened MSW programs. BSWs will not be able to continue to be mini-MSWs. What BSWs need is a regimen of knowledge, attitudes, and skills that is commensurate with the specialist functions assigned to the BSW. Whether the BSW degree can be a way station on the road to the MSW should be considered a secondary but not a primary question.

Third, educational experimentation should proceed from the recognition that the several academic degrees now in existence in social work education are part of an educational system. Changes in one will produce changes in the other. Neither the direction nor the content of the MSW program is engraved in stone. Since the MSW specialist is viewed as the key practitioner, albeit not the only one in the schema suggested here, it behooves the profession to consider what educational preparations the MSW candidate requires. If a variety of specialist practitioners are needed, the MSW should continue to be considered as the degree for practitioners and the doctorate as the degree for persons equipped to develop and create knowledge. If the profession decides that a doctorate is a more appropriate terminal point for the practitioner specialist because such practice requires increased depth and breadth, then the profession's model should be the MD or the JD. The Ph.D. should then continue to serve as the degree for those who wish to embark on careers of knowledge development and research. Such a position would lead to upgrading the MSW degree as it now exists. The profession should not flinch from such a course if, upon careful thought and in the light of debate, it appears wise and practicable.

Summary

This paper attempts to create a framework for professional practice that could serve as a guide for empirical studies of the functions of both BSW and MSW professional personnel. In this framework, social work has a place not only in the personal social services and other traditional roles, but also in other social institutions and programs, such as health and mental health organizations, income maintenance programs, housing and urban renewal programs, educational institutions, and judicial and correctional institutions.

In traditional social welfare programs, the MSWs can continue to perform the key roles in the assessment and design of intervention strategies as well as the monitoring role for all aspects of the intervention process. In addition, MSWs can function as supervisors and consultants, and they can assume responsibilities as managers and administrators, planners and coordinators, and social policy technicians in all social institutions with social welfare components.

A specialist role has also been identified for the BSW, that of an implementer, of a participant in all aspects of the intervention including evaluation. As much as possible, all such functions should be carried out under the tutelage of the MSW who has overall responsibility. The role of generalist often prescribed for the BSW is impracticable. The functions identified for the BSW include such roles as provider in the delivery of services, facilitator of access, advocate and evaluator of outcome, and these functions can be carried out in any social institution with a social welfare component.

These suggestions are no more than hypotheses for manpower deployment, hypotheses that beckon to be tested. The article also considers the implications of such a specialist-oriented deployment pattern for social work education.

Notes and References

1. Werner W. Boehm, *Social Casework*, 60 (February 1979), pp. 119–121. *See also* Betty L. Baer and Ronald Federico, *Educating the Baccalaureate Social Worker* (Cambridge, Mass.: Ballinger Publishing Co., 1978).

2. Arnold Gurin, "Education for Changing Practice," in Alfred S. Kahn, ed., *Shaping the New Social Work* (New York: Columbia University Press, 1973), p. 171.

3. Harriett Bartlett, *The Common Base of Social Work Practice* (New York: National Association of Social Workers, 1970); and Elliot Studt, "Social Work Theory and Implications for the Practice of the Methods," *Social Work Education Reporter*, 16 (June 1968), pp. 22–46. *See also* William E. Gordon, "A Critique of the Working Definition," *Social Work*, 7 (October 1962), pp. 3–13.

4. For an earlier formulation of the five P's, *see* Werner W. Boehm, "The Core of the Social Work Curriculum" (New Brunswick, N. J.: Graduate School of Social Work, Rutgers University, 1977). (Mimeographed.) *See also* Werner W. Boehm, "Continuum in Education for Social Work," in Edward J. Muller, James R. Dumpson, and Associates, eds., *Evaluation of Social Intervention* (San Francisco: Jossey-Bass, 1972), pp. 213–239.

5. Bartlett, op. cit., pp. 62–69.

6. Ibid., p. 116.

7. *See* Werner W. Boehm, "Common and Specific Learnings for a Graduate of a School of Social Work," *Journal of Education for Social Work*, 4 (Fall 1968), p. 17, and "Human Well-Being," in *Proceedings of the Nineteenth International Conference on Social Welfare* (New York: Columbia University Press, 1979), pp. 138–143.

8. For a summary of current developments regarding the concept of pre-

vention and its usefulness in social work practice, *see* Milton Wittman, "Preventive Social Work," *Encyclopedia of Social Work*, Vol. 2 (Washington, D.C.: National Association of Social Workers, 1977), pp. 1049–1053.

9. Bartlett, op. cit.

10. Ibid. *See also* William E. Gordon, "Toward a Social Work Frame of Reference," *Social Work*, 10 (July 1965), pp. 19–26.

11. Werner W. Boehm, "The Nature of Social Work," *Social Work* 3 (April 1958), pp. 10–18, and "Toward New Models of Social Work Practice," *Social Work Practice, 1967: Proceedings of the National Conference on Social Welfare* (New York: Columbia University Press, 1967), pp. 3–18.

12. Arnold Gurin, op. cit., p. 196.

13. On the variety of services appropriately allocated to BSW personnel, *see Undergraduate Social Work Education for Practice*, Vols. 1 and 2 (Washington, D.C.: Veterans Administration, 1971); and Baer and Federico, op. cit.

14. *See* Robert L. Barker and Thomas L. Briggs, *Differential Use of Social Work Manpower* (New York: National Association of Social Workers, 1968). *See also* Barker and Briggs, *Using Teams to Deliver Social Services* (Syracuse, N.Y.: Syracuse University, 1969); and Dorothy Bird Daly, "New Ways and New Potentials for Social Work Man Power Development," *1968 Annual Review* (New York: National Commission for Social Work Careers, 1968).

15. *See* Richard Enos, "Undergraduate Social Work Manpower and Job Opportunities: A Regional Study," *Journal of Education for Social Work*, 14 (Fall 1978), pp. 34–41.

16. Anne Minahan and Allen Pincus, "Conceptual Framework for Social Work Practice," *Social Work*, 22 (September 1977), pp. 347–352. *See also* Werner W. Boehm, "Toward New Models of Social Work Practice."

14

The Centrality of Social Work in the Mental Health Services

Milton Wittman

The organization and functioning of mental health services have changed considerably in recent decades, as has what social workers do in mental health services. This article reviews the history of social work in mental health from 1905 to 1979, emphasizing the changing role and status of social work in recent years, assessing the impact of two major recent reports, and analyzing the central issues confronting social work education and practice in mental health. The pervading themes of the article are the crisis of community care for the mentally ill and the need during the coming decade for a public health program that will address the mental health needs of the whole population.

The first social workers to be employed in psychiatric hospitals were assigned to positions in Boston and New York hospitals in 1905.[1] Deutsch states that the first social worker to work in a state mental hospital was Miss E. H. Horton, who was employed in 1906 by the Manhattan State Hospital under the auspices of the New York State Charities Aid Association.[2] She provided social histories and undertook family liaison functions. Miss Horton's pattern of services emerged twelve years later, at the end of World War I, as the field of psychiatric social work, one of several categorical groups among the many that came into being between the world wars. This field produced a lively organization called the American Association of Psychiatric Social

Workers, which did much to advance standards for practice and education. It insisted on the need for two full years of postgraduate education for the master's degree in social work.

In 1940, a major national study, undertaken and published with the help of the Commonwealth Fund, estimated that there were eleven hundred psychiatric social workers. This study also reported on the distribution of psychiatric social workers in psychiatric hospitals and mental health clinics, in social work education, and in mental health education.[3] Disparity between the number of psychiatric social workers available and the estimated need has always been large, but the gap was closed considerably by the implementation of the National Mental Health Act of 1946. In 1950 there were twenty-six approved training programs in psychiatric social work, and at that time the National Institute of Mental Health estimated that from thirteen to fifteen thousand social workers would be needed to staff "existing and planned programs."[4] In 1976, the National Center for Health Statistics was able to report a total of 31,200 social workers in psychiatric settings.[5]

The 1963 Community Mental Health and Mental Retardation Centers Act, which was amended in 1965 and 1975, stimulated the development of new programs that attracted large numbers of qualified social workers. In 1976, 6,752 social workers were employed in Community Mental Health Centers.[6] This amounted to 13.9 percent of full-time staff and compared with 9.5 percent for registered nurses, 9.4 percent for psychologists, and 4.7 for psychiatrists. The same report indicated that, for all mental health facilities, social workers are found in greater numbers than psychiatrists and psychologists—6.1 percent compared to 3.6 percent for each of the other groups.

It is clear, therefore, that the mental health field has long attracted social workers and that these professionals have carried a good share of the patient load in community service facilities. The American Association of Psychiatric Social Workers, which became part of the National Association of Social Workers (NASW) in 1955, had a strong tradition of service to the mentally ill and their families and consistently exhibited concern for advancing the standards of education and practice.[7] After 1955 the Psychiatric Social Work Section of the unified National Association of Social Workers undertook a number of conferences and studies aimed at clarifying and explicating the role and functions of the social worker in mental health.[8] With the change in 1963 in the structure of social work specializations, the section became the Council on Social Work in Psychiatric and Mental Health Services. This organization faltered because of a lack of funding and because the national association shifted its emphasis away from the specialized interests of different groups in the profession. Psychiatric social workers found means for advancing their interests in organizations such as the Society for Clinical Social Workers, the Conference of Social Workers in State and Territorial Mental Health Programs, the Social Work Section of the American Public Health Association. However, none of these organizations met all the needs of the social workers in mental health.

Division of Labor

In recent years the Council on Social Work Education (CSWE) has undertaken a number of initiatives to develop research data and to obtain national and regional assessments of policy issues in community mental health. One study, that of the Community Mental Health Practice-Education Project, gathered data from 135 agencies and nine schools of social work.[9] Of particular interest were the findings regarding the division of labor between baccalaureate-level and master's-level social workers. The study examined the distribution of twenty direct service functions in social work and mental health, obtaining responses from 1,352 workers with masters' in social work and 531 baccalaureate-level staff. The MSW group had greater involvement in such functions as long-term intensive psychotherapy and case management; the BA staff provided more of the concrete services and home visiting. The involvement of BA staff in such activities as short-term treatment and crisis intervention was similar to that of the MSW group. These findings paralleled those of an earlier study carried out in Chicago which had found that although workers with master's degrees were handling the more complex aspects of patient care, some non-MSW workers had similar responsibilities.[10] This study provided the foundation for an approach to education for work in community mental health that led one graduate school to undertake the preparation of a mental health generalist.[11]

Over the years the core of clinical services that workers provide in mental health has broadened to include administration, community organization, consultation, research, and teaching.[12] A controversial aspect of preparation for service in community mental health has emerged in the specialized programs in community organization and advocacy that sometimes do not require clinical experience.[13] The preference of most leaders in the field is that social workers preparing to work in community mental health have some clinical training or experience before undertaking the nonclinical aspects of this service. Ozarin, who coordinates rural mental health activities for the National Institute of Mental Health (NIMH), favors a background in clinical skills for persons who work in mental health consultation and community development in rural communities.[14]

The CSWE curriculum study reported by Rubin presented some important data and conclusions about variations in the organization of the MSW-level mental health curriculum. In the late 1970s, some schools of social work emphasized concentration in specialized areas of the mental health curriculum; others offered a diffusion of content throughout the curriculum. The report notes that although all students were exposed to an extensive range of content related to community mental health, "in most schools, those identified as concentrating on [community mental health] tended to focus on knowledge and skills associated with clinical diagnosis and treatment methods in direct service delivery."[15]

There was, moreover, a pervasive strain between the "ecological" approach and the "psychotherapeutic forms of mental health practice."[16] Faculty and students both reported that a central objective for many students was a career in treatment rather than in community service, and the study reported that "most mental health field settings and field supervisors used in each type of [graduate-level] program were ... primarily interested in psychotherapeutic forms of treatment."[17]

In a recent CSWE monograph, Katz reviews the issues in the clinical-community controversy.[18] There is a growing restlessness with the dominance of the medical model in mental health services, and this has been reflected in efforts to limit the appointment of psychiatrists as directors of mental health centers. More social workers than psychiatrists are now appointed as directors. This change occurred between 1971 and 1976 when the proportion of psychiatrist directors dropped from 55.3 to 30 percent, and the number of social work directors increased from 11 to 31.3 percent.[19]

Katz's approach to this issue is practical. He sees both medical practice and human services practice as ideological models in the system of community mental health services. The tendency of psychiatrists to see mental health under the general domain of health is supported by the medical model. However, the principal target population and the main concern of government and legislatures is the mentally ill person in the community. Thus the human services system becomes essential to adequate community services. Katz correctly points to the current problems in the definition of specialization in social work and to the uncertainty about the true scope of community mental health as deterrents to consensus on the division of labor and locus of authority for central direction and planning on state and national levels.

Despite the increasing number of federal laws in the past decade, there is still confusion about how health services will be organized at the state and regional levels, about how to maintain quality controls, and, most important, about how the community mental health programs will be financed.[20] The mandate for better organization and more complete coverage of all populations will eventually come from the consumer, who will ask for an end to the interminable rivalries and bootless competition that stand in the way of effective service delivery at the local level, which is where it counts the most.

The Next Decade

To sense the direction of mental health services in the 1980s, it is necessary to look at two reports that emerged in 1978 as a direct result of the initiatives of the Carter administration. The President's Commission on Mental Health, with the president's wife, Mrs. Rosalynn Carter, as honorary chairperson, produced a final report and three volumes of task panel reports that have had a considerable impact on research, training, and services in mental health.[21] One direct result of the commission's work was the Illinois Mental Health Code of 1978, which was the first to create flexible guidelines for admissions to mental hospitals.

The formation of the Department of Health, Education and Welfare Task Force on Implementation was a natural consequence of the report of the president's commission. From May until December 1978, a cross-discipline group worked on two main objectives: "to identify and analyze the implications for HEW programs [of the report of the president's commission] . . . and to propose legislative, budgetary, administrative, or programmatic actions for the Department that would be responsive to the Commission's recommendations and intent."[22] The final report of the task force dealt with social and community supports, services, financing, personnel, basic rights, knowledge development, prevention, and public understanding.

Apart from the budgetary impact of increased allocations for research and services, the most important outcome of the task force report was the proposal for the Mental Health Systems Act of 1980.[23] This act, if passed and funded, would revolutionize the infrastructure of community services for the mentally ill. The act would implement a major recommendation of the President's Commission on Mental Health and expand the excellent projects carried out on a demonstration basis under the NIMH Community Support Program.[24] The act would provide substantial impetus to improving long-term care and give renewed emphasis to primary prevention. The act would also move toward implementing long-needed coordination of mental health and human services programs, and the proposed linkage mechanism has promise for reducing bureaucratic obstacles to bringing together the services of community health and mental health centers.

The import of the Mental Health Systems Act for social work and social services is substantial. The projects to demonstrate how the Community Support Program works at the state and local levels clearly involve substantial social work participation. Further, the proposed act calls for comprehensiveness, universality of coverage, accessibility of services, improved coordination, expanded preventive activities, continuity of care, humanity in approach, attention to the underserved and unserved, and community involvement. Services to minorities are given particular emphasis.

Although social work has a commanding lead in the training and development of Black mental health specialists, much more remains to be done if the needs of inner city populations are to be met.[25] The same could be said about any of the minorities of color in the United States. Although work to help the Asian–Pacific Islander population on the West Coast was under way in 1973, it was not until 1977 that a project was funded in the New York Chinatown to further the training of bilingual staff for seriously understaffed services. Programs to develop social work manpower among American Indians are just beginning to produce graduates who can carry out research and teaching as well as direct services. The Chicano and Puerto Rican communities reflect a vast dissatisfaction over the decline in support and lack of regional recognition that has occurred in recent years. Other ethnic populations that are less visible and not vocal have received little attention. Those in rural enclaves of poverty are particularly vulnerable. A recent book on the rural poor was well entitled *Roots of Futility*.[26] This careful and detailed study of mothers of abused or neglected children verified the bad fit between welfare and mental health programs. Community support is needed not for the chronic mental patient alone.

The second major study that sets a direction for community mental health in the 1980s is the report of a special Manpower Policy Analysis Task Force. This study is a useful companion to the report of the

President's Commission on Mental Health because it represents an attempt by a newly appointed administrator of the Alcohol, Drug Abuse, and Mental Health Administration (ADAMHA) to understand and correct a perplexing problem in American mental health services—the persistent deficit, after more than thirty years of program development, in the mental health manpower available to rural and minority populations.[27] Central issues of the study were the supply, distribution, and utilization of manpower for the three categorical national institutes concerned with problems of alcohol, drugs, and mental health. The report is the result of a cluster of survey and study methods that used a panel of expert consultants drawn from the core mental health disciplines and included advocates for paraprofessional workers as well. The final report contained twenty-one major policy and program recommendations, thirty-two legislative recommendations, and seventy-three detailed recommendations related to specific issues, problems, and needs. The report emphasized the deficits in rural areas, in minority manpower, and in services for the aged, for children and youth, for the physically handicapped, and for the chronically mentally ill patient in the community. This repeated the message of the President's Commission on Mental Health, a message likely to become a prevailing force for change if the Carter administration is able to achieve its health and mental health objectives.

Credentials and Licensing

The 1979 issue of *Health Resources Statistics* described two types of credentialing: recognizing the competence of educational programs to prepare personnel (accreditation), and recognizing the competence of individuals to deliver services (certification, registration or association membership, and licensure).[28] Accreditation of schools of social work education at the MSW and BSW levels is the responsibility of the Council on Social Work Education. Beginning with the establishment of the Academy of Certified Social Workers in 1961, NASW has promoted the credentialing of social workers. In 1964, NASW affirmed support of a policy to promote state licensing, and in 1974 it introduced a model statute along with a policy statement on the legal regulation of social work practice.[29] The NASW model identified four levels of practice: social work associate (AA and BA), social worker (BSW), certified social workers (MSW), and independent practitioner (MSW plus two years of specialized experience). Social work licensure has continued to face problems, however. Although NASW lists about half the states as licensing social workers, Hardcastle pointed out the laws in none of these states provide "functional exclusiveness" for social work or establish clear criteria for educational requirements and entrance examinations.[30] This has become a serious question in Maryland, where the state's law has been interpreted as pertaining to certification of title rather than to licensure of function. Thus Maryland's State Board of Social Work Examiners is faced with the prospect of revisions that will run counter to the model statute. Since the Board of Directors of NASW recently reaffirmed the eight "essential elements" in the model statute, an interesting contest lies ahead for the continuity of the licensure program.

Full licensure will require the accurate and comprehensive identification of the functions of social work practice. Should these functions be seen as existing only in clinical practice? The Academy of Certified Social Workers' certificate is provided to qualified persons in all areas of social work practice. Admission to NASW's *Register of Clinical Social Workers* is clearly limited to those with clinical qualifications. The link between licensure and vendorship payments is obvious, and it becomes critically important for social workers to develop a clear and convincing statement of social work functions that will be admissible and acceptable for purposes of licensure. Although universal licensing is far off, the drive for nationwide coverage should continue.

Major Issues

Some perplexing and frustrating problems must be faced by social workers in the near future. They emerge from close scrutiny of the many recommendations and proposals found in the reports of the President's Commission on Mental Health and the ADAMHA task force. They also arise from the old social work problem of status and recognition, which finds social workers facing state declassification actions that are clearly aimed at reducing the costs of services. This cost-benefit thrust has been felt in mental health programs.

The bitter debate to locate responsibility for the neglect of mental patients in the community invariably involves all social workers in the social agency and human services networks regardless of educational level. An NASW conference on declassification provided a means for communication on this issue.[31] The present crisis derives in part from the recognition in 1969 of the BSW social worker as part of the professional fabric of social work. Although there have been many studies of the division of labor between BSW and MSW social workers, none has yet definitively established the differences. The evolving role of the case manager in the community support system is a good illustration of the complexities that beset this question. The case manager role is a concept that is gaining currency, but the role is a multidimensional one that still lacks well established forms of training, deployment, and continuing education.

A task for social work is to look closely at what might emerge if the Mental Health Systems Act becomes law. Elements of the proposed legislation will expand the community support network, extend prevention programs, and enlarge the linkages between health and mental health. The act thus emphasizes the psychosocial aspect of mental illness, which has been a long-standing preoccupation of social workers regardless of specialty, level of training, or role in service delivery. The relationship of an illness to the family, the group, and the community is critical to the person who is or has been ill. Such psychosocial matters determine the degree to which a former patient has access to a satisfactory life. They also have direct bearing on the quality of life of the person who has never been hospitalized and who, with minimal support, is capable of living outside the institution. Social work, moreover, must develop new modes for community care and evaluate them for their utility in the present family and agency configurations. Finally, social work, in carrying out its mission in the mental health field, must reaffirm its long-standing, parallel commitment to human welfare.

Notes and References

1. Leon Lucas, "Psychiatric Social Work," in Margaret B. Hodges, ed., *Social Work Year Book,* (New York: National Association of Social Workers, 1951), pp. 359–365.

2. Albert Deutsch, *The Mentally Ill in America* (New York: Columbia University Press, 1949), p. 290.

3. Lois M. French, *Psychiatric Social Work* (New York: Commonwealth Fund, 1940).

4. Lucas, op. cit., p. 363.

5. Office of Health Research, Statistics and Technology, Department of Health, Education and Welfare, "Social Work," in *Health Resources Statistics: 1976–1977* (Washington, D.C.: U.S. Government Printing Office, 1979), pp. 247–252.

6. National Institute of Mental Health, *Community Mental Health Centers: The Federal Investment* (Washington, D.C.: U.S. Government Printing Office, 1978), p. 36.

7. Tessie D. Berkman, *Practice of Social Workers in Psychiatric Hospitals and Clinics* (New York: American Association of Psychiatric Social Workers, 1952); and Ruth I. Knee, ed., *Better Social Services for Mentally Ill Patients* (New York: American Association of Psychiatric Social Workers, 1955).

8. Gordon J. Aldridge, ed., *Social Issues and Psychiatric Social Work Practice,* and Luther E. Woodward, ed., *Psychiatric Social Workers and Mental Health* (New York: National Association of Social Workers, 1961).

9. Mary G. Harm, ed., *A Report of the Community Mental Health Practice-Education Project* (New York: Council on Social Work Education, 1978).

10. Lawrence K. Berg, William J. Reid, and Stephen Z. Cohen, *Social Workers in Community Mental Health* (Chicago, Ill.: University of Chicago School of Social Service Administration, 1972).

11. Allen Rubin, *Community Mental Health in the Social Work Curriculum* (New York: Council on Social Work Education, 1979), pp. 29–31.

12. Neilson F. Smith and Milton Wittman, "New Roles and Services in the Community Mental Health Center," in Felice D. Perlmutter, ed., *A Design for Social Work Practice* (New York: Columbia University Press, 1974), pp. 79–100.

13. John B. Turner, *Roles for Social Work in Community Mental Health Programs* (Columbus, Ohio: National Conference on Social Welfare, 1977).

14. Personal communication from Lucy D. Ozarin, Division of Mental Health Service Programs, National Institutite of Mental Health, Rockville, Md., April 18, 1979.

15. Rubin, op. cit., p. 48.

16. Ibid., p. 24.

17. Ibid., p. 27.

18. Arthur J. Katz, ed., *Community Mental Health: Issues for Social Work Practice and Education* (New York: Council on Social Work Education, 1979).

19. National Institute of Mental Health, op. cit., p. 41.

20. Milton Wittman, "New Directions for Social Work in Mental Health," in Francine Sobey, ed., *Changing Roles in Social Work Practice* (Philadelphia, Pa.: Temple University Press, 1977), pp. 72–91.

21. *Report to the President from the President's Commission on Mental Health* (Washington, D.C.: U.S. Government Printing Office, 1978).

22. Department of Health, Education and Welfare, *Task Force on the Report to the President from the President's Commission on Mental Health* (Washington, D.C.: U.S. Government Printing Office, 1979), p. 1.

23. U.S. Congress, Senate and House, "Mental Health Systems Act, 1980," S. 1177 and H.R. 4156, *Congressional Record,* May 17, 1979, pp. 36158–36169.

24. Judith Turner and William J. TenHoor, "The NIMH Community Support Program: Pilot Approach to a Needed Social Reform," *Schizophrenia,* 4 (1978), pp. 319–348.

25. *See* Willie S. Williams, James C. Ralph, and William H. Denham, "Black Mental Health Work Force," in Lawrence E. Gary, ed., *Mental Health: A Challenge to the Black Community* (Philadelphia, Pa.: Dorrance & Co., 1978), pp. 294–313.

26. Norman A. Polansky, Robert D. Borgman, and Christine De Saix, *Roots of Futility* (San Francisco: Jossey-Bass, 1972).

27. *Report of the Alcohol, Drug Abuse and Mental Health Administration Manpower Analysis Task Force,* Vols. 1 and 2 (Rockville, Md.: Alcohol, Drug Abuse and Mental Health Administration, 1978).

28. National Center for Health Statistics, *Health Resources Statistics* (Washington, D.C.: U.S. Government Printing Office, 1979), pp. 6–7.

29. "New Policy on Licensing Issued," *NASW News,* 19 (September 1974), pp. 12–24.

30. David A. Hardcastle, "Public Regulation of Social Work," *Social Work,* 22 (January 1977), pp. 14–20. For a response to Hardcastle's views, *see* Myles Johnson, "Points and Viewpoints," *Social Work,* 22 (March 1977), pp. 87 and 140.

31. *Proceedings of the National Conference on the Validation of Social Work Classifications, Colorado Springs, Colorado, April 24–26, 1977* (Washington, D.C.: National Association of Social Workers, 1977).

15

Shaping New Methodologies

Shirley Cooper

Methods of social work cannot be considered apart from the context, concepts, and climate that surround the profession. The pressing and complex influences that currently bear on emerging methodologies include (1) the hurtling pace of change, (2) the values abroad in the nation, particularly those that influence attitudes about human services and shape social policy, (3) fiscal and program supports or stringencies, (4) social problems that capture focus and concern, (5) the pressures and forces diverse groups mobilize to capture attention, (6) the means different groups in the population use in their attempts to solve problems or adapt, and (7) the theories and concepts developed to guide the formation of new methods and skills. These forces interact with each other, and although this list is certainly not exhaustive, these are powerful influences dictating the methodology of social work. Some of these influences require closer scrutiny.

Although people weary of hearing that these final decades of the twentieth century are singularly marked by change, this phenomenon of relentless, rapid change nevertheless profoundly influences everyone's efforts and attitudes. Within a few decades, more massive changes have occurred in the conditions of people's lives than in all previous millenia. Although tradition can encase people in outworn beliefs, it can also guide values and behavior. For a time, the system of tradition and belief that seemed to meet modern needs most was science. Although according science its due as contributing significantly to mankind's capacity to gain vast control over the environment, Frank nevertheless comments,

> Science easily becomes perverted into scientism—*faith* in the scientific
> method as not only the solution to problems, but also as a generator of
> values. . . . It is clear now that [scientism] is a Pied Piper luring humanity
> down the path of destruction by dazzling it with endless goodies.[1]

Yet science brought with it a true explosion of knowledge and a
pressing need for specialists and specialization, which also proved to be
a two-edged sword. Specialization can help to produce a more profoundly educated and skilled person able to render more effective
help. However, specializations can also create narrow perspectives,
foreshorten vision, and produce partisanship and fragmentation. Social
work is once again moving toward specializations, and whether these
will lead to a true and coherent pluralism or to further divisiveness and
conflict remains in doubt.

Although we social workers have difficulty arriving at a consensus on
any issue, we can all agree that the present trend of events and the
values currently abroad in this land make these dreary times for human
services. Inflation erodes the standard of living for large sections of the
population, and it bites most heavily into the basic necessities of life—
food, housing, health care, and energy. In 1934, corporate taxes ac-
counted for 44 percent of the national budget. By 1979 that figure had
shrunk to 14 percent.[2] It is not accidental that in such a climate a tax
revolt developed influencing attitudes about human services and about
the funding necessary to insure their delivery.

In the author's own city, San Francisco, Proposition 13 and the
Proposition 13 mentality that has swept California led in 1979 to a
reduction of $4.3 million for mental health services. This occurred
even though the day the state legislature terminated its session, a $1.3
billion surplus was discovered. The result of the fiscal reduction was
that the city's major inpatient services for children and adolescents
were cut by half and several inpatient adult wards were closed, making
it impossible at times to hospitalize even seriously suicidal or homicidal
patients and creating severe overcrowding in the jail ward. In addition,
there were sharp reductions in outpatient and partial care mental
health services throughout the city. Some agencies closed cases pre-
cipitously in spite of obvious and continued need, and other programs
were terminated completely. In the Department of Psychiatry at Mt.
Zion Medical Center, several major programs were closed, including a
family crisis program that had been acknowledged as a model of prevention and intervention for at-risk children and families.

Examples abound in every field to illustrate how social policy and its
fiscal accompaniments dictate the manner in which services will or will

not be organized and delivered. The methods used in delivering these services are also influenced. Brief treatment is not now a method of choice, dictated by practice judgments about clients' circumstances; it is often the only method fiscal stringencies permit. Of course, brief, focal, or task-oriented casework was at times dictated by theoretical persuasions, sometimes appropriately and sometimes not. However, such choices and considerations based on methodological predilections or on thorough contextual assessments of what might be most appropriate may now be blocked by the buck.

Getting Attention

Another major influence bearing on methodology derives from the problems and issues that capture attention and concern. Increased mobility, changing relationships between men and women, changing attitudes about sex and marriage, and changing economic, social, and environmental circumstances have sharply influenced family life and the rate of divorce. Between 1970 and 1976, the rate of divorce tripled in the United States, and the percentage of children under 18 living in one-parent families doubled. It is no accident that divorce counseling has become a prominent social work intervention and that ways of intervening in changing family and child-rearing patterns are evolving and new ways are being sought. Nor is it accidental that family therapy has become a far more prevalent form of practice. At times, necessity is the mother of invention, but, as Frank asserts, "it may also be the parent of nihilism."[3]

As the American population grows older, the aged have come into society's awareness, and attention properly turns to serving this group. The impersonal abstractions of demographics become living problems. A hundred years ago, only 1 or 2 percent of the population was over 65; today, there are some twenty million over 65, representing a little over 10 percent of the population. By the year 2000, the elderly may comprise 15 percent of the nation. Fifty years ago in Massachusetts, one-half of all households included at least one adult besides the parents. Today, the figure is 4 percent.[4]

Not only are the aged and the aging a larger proportion of the total population than ever before, they are also better educated and less frail than previous generations, and they have become a vocal group, calling attention to their needs. A variety of factors influence the quality of life for aging citizens. Women live longer than men and are often isolated and lonely. (Contributing to female longevity is the rate of male homicide and suicide; among males between the ages of 15 through 24, suicide is the third leading cause of death, a rate three times higher than twenty-five years ago.[5]) Now that the nuclear family finds no space physically or psychologically for multigenerational living, housing and economic factors often add special burdens for the aged.

As each new group with its special interests and problems captures social work's attention, the profession begins to consider ways of meeting that group's needs. Two simultaneous trends seem to be emerging in social work efforts with the aging. The profession has focused attention on developing varied services for the aged, combining health, recreation, housing, and counseling services, and it has set about acquiring the new skills needed to deliver these services. The profession has also identified as requiring assistance the children of aged parents, although, until recently, there has been more lip service than true concern for this group. At the same time, a tendency to romanticize the aging process has emerged in the profession. Perhaps this occurs as a corrective to prejudice, but the antidote to ageism does not lie in romanticizing and idealizing—a process as distorting as bias.

As the needs of additional groups become clear, the profession is forced to turn to specialization. The field of social work is now so vast that no one can master all the knowledge and acquire all the skills inherent in its many parts. In the 1960s and 1970s, there was an explosion of practice styles, and too often and too soon they became enshrined as new practice theories or new methodologies. A single mode of intervention aimed at a single goal is not a new theory, nor a new practice, nor a full specialization. Nor is the delineation of a separate area of interest necessarily the soundest approach to conceptualizing a specialty.

The field of child abuse is a case in point. During the 1970s, at the same time that programs to address this important problem were springing up everywhere, the rate of homicide for children under a year nearly doubled. Only later did these figures decline somewhat. Some of this rise may be attributed to better identification and reporting, but one must acknowledge that although the family remains the most vital force for socialization, it has also become the society's most violent institution.

Social work methods alone cannot deal with the problem of family violence or child abuse, yet it cannot be overlooked that the profession's methodological interventions and program conceptions in these areas remain primitive. The early allure for so many child abuse programs of advocacy, education, identification, and mandatory reporting has dimmed. These approaches have not truly addressed the problem, and Teberg's study bears this assessment out. Working with thirty-one teen-age mothers and their infants, Teberg and her group discovered an alarming number of disturbing social and emotional behaviors in al-most two-thirds of the mothers and their infants. Despite the extensive home advocacy program mounted to assist these young people, the results were depressingly unsuccessful.[6]

It is fitting that social workers search for new practice skills. Siporin comments that

> there have been a series of infatuations (virtually promiscuous in nature) with varied hues and persuasions of approaches to practice. These include therapies called transactional analysis, gestalt, encounter group, rational-emotive, behavior modification, structural and systems family, bioenergetic, feminist, sex, zen, TM, and Arica.

This listing is not inclusive, and Siporin adds,

> It is wondrous to behold the many social workers who flock excitedly to successively avant-garde types of seminars, workshops and study groups, and who then return home to report ecstatically about their new wondrous techniques, until the next trip. Also, there is an effort to accumulate new techniques, piling the new upon the old in a wild kind of eclecticism that gives the appearance of thoughtless ignorance and inconsistent, illogical self-contradictions.[7]

Meyer comments persuasively that "an encyclopedia of meth-odologies placed end to end has not proved capable of successfully expressing and putting to work social work values, knowledge, and purposes in an accountable way."[8] She argues cogently for a contextual perspective instead of the constraining methodological one, insisting with Bartlett that the profession's methods must become the servants rather than the masters of its practice activities.

Practice driven by purist methodological adherence has been a major weakness in social work and a source of divisiveness. The author's urging that practitioners expand their horizons to consider program designs, that they assess needs carefully, and that they delineate con-cepts to address those needs with diverse and inventive methods stands close to Meyer's thinking.[9] Meyer urges social workers to formulate conceptual or geographic boundaries and to assess and address all the issues within such boundaries.[10] Program conceptions are an attempt to put into operation such an ecological perspective, which is urged upon social work by such important social work thinkers as Germain and Maluccio.[11]

The profession has not only been confined by methodological

rigidities; theoretical rigidities have also restricted development. Doctrinaire attachments to one or another theoretical perspective obscures the reality that the theories to explain human behavior are largely metaphors that cannot as yet dictate precisely, clearly, and thoroughly which methods should be used.[12] Theories of behavior, as so many writers indicate, are on a level of abstraction that defy translations into sound actions. Nor will an atheoretical or antitheoretical posture take social work where it must go. The so-called spontaneity often turns to recklessness at the expense of order, coherence, and replication.

Adapting Theory to Practice

Fraiberg has often spoken of the impatience social work has shown in discarding theoretical perspectives that may have great utility. She asserts that social work has failed to harvest the potential inherent in psychodynamic concepts about human behavior and in the circumstances of people's lives. Since Fraiberg's recent work bears centrally on social work methodology, it is worth discussing in detail. At a conference in 1979, she described and illustrated her work with eight of the most impaired of her fifty-five mother-infant pairs.[13] These 16- to 18-year-old mothers were born into poverty and supported by welfare; they were living without supports apart from family, depressed and alone. All eight teenagers had difficulty with their mothers, and their backgrounds and circumstances documented once again what social workers see all too often—the endless, unbroken cycle of despairing multigenerational disorder. These young mothers and their failing-to-thrive infants challenge every ounce of skill and knowledge social workers possess.

Fraiberg and her colleagues became the interpreters for the infants' powerful, although yet unsuccessful efforts to engage their parents in mutual pleasure and attachment. In turn, these attachments unleash a new capacity for self-love in the mother, awakening responses in her and setting in motion a healing, reciprocal relationship for both partners. It is in understanding the electrifying power of attachment—knowing how attachments are ruptured and can be restored, if the work occurs soon enough—that progression is fostered and healing facilitated.

Central to this work are patience, the avoidance of blame, and an individualized understanding of the unresolved conflicts in attachment these young parents derive from their mothers and from their often idealized, unknown, or unavailable fathers.

Uncovering rivalries displaced on the infant and offering consistent reflection that the infant and the helper see the young parent as the most significant and wanted person in the baby's life gradually bring about changes for these mothers and their babies. Further, these workers make every effort to intervene in the conditions of their clients' lives, assisting with nutrition, health care, and all manner of environmental factors. Documented on film, the evidence is inescapable that the workers have helped a large group of clients significantly. Fraiberg's audience watched raptly as a listless, developmentally lagging, silent, undernourished, and detached 7-month-old began to emerge as an animated, vocalizing, engaged, and engaging 11-month-old. At 24 months, this toddler and her mother seemed like new people, although the mother continued to have problems.

The work is rooted in fundamental principles of casework, steeped in the concept of self-determination, and built on sophisticated acceptance and the most careful individualized assessment of the clients and the circumstances in which they live. Dynamic understanding is not used primarily to develop insight, but to build a relationship between mother, infant, and helper, and this relationship becomes the basis for a totally new experience for these teenage mothers: they are seen as valued, important, and unmatched, and this experience drastically alters their self-regard.

The theoretical underpinnings of this work do not lie exclusively in social work. They rest heavily on developmental and dynamic concepts and are steeped in newly emerging understandings of infant development, attachment and object theory, separation and individuation, the psychology of narcissism, and the psychology of the self. This blending of highly sophisticated psychological concepts with concepts of outreach, early intervention, home visits, advocacy, environmental interventions, work with families as an interactional unit, and attention to the poor are what the best of social work is all about. No other helping profession has accepted as fully as social work the mandate to work with people and the conditions of their lives.

What does this work teach? On one level, it is a reminder to become ever more clear in differentiating general conditions that may impair from specific conditions which do impair. Poverty and social, physical, and psychological stress do not in themselves breed disorder. Alert to the potential of such conditions for intensifying or sustaining problems, social workers must become more skillful in understanding why some succumb and others transcend potentially traumatic conditions.

Fraiberg's work further teaches social workers that even now, while theoretical understanding remains imperfect, it is possible to distill conceptual principles to guide method. The fit between theory and practice then becomes possible and specific. This work offers us a model for linking casework with research about interventions.

Contrast Fraiberg's work with the many programs that address child welfare. The designs with which the author is familiar often provide the most superficial assistance, offer but minimal respite, or end with child placement. Fundamental relationships between parent and child often remain basically unaffected. Some designs do reduce overt abuse, but this frequently mutes into abandonment or neglect as the mothers continue to experience their children as burdens rather than as sources of joy and pride.

Promising New Directions

There are hopeful and positive signs. Social workers are learning largely from sociologists that alienated and detached families breed difficulty and discord. Various program models are developing that show promise of helping people find supportive networks. Although many of these networks have developed from self-help groups, social workers are beginning to consider an array of preventive and interventive styles and methods to counter alienation.[14]

There is a revolution under way in the field of child welfare. Here the professionals have been badly battered. The early promise of foster care has turned sour, but child welfare workers are becoming far wiser in recognizing that surrogate care for children has its own hazards and cannot be taken lightly. However, this hard-won understanding is unfortunately not matched by the resources necessary to stave off family disruptions. There are hazards to child welfare's new understanding. Permanency planning, family reunification, and adoption are important and viable alternatives to child placement, but they can be misapplied, as in the case of a 12-year-old boy who had been a subject in a study aimed at family reunification. With undaunted inventiveness, the workers searched out the mother who had placed her child in a foster home when he was 6 months of age; she was then 15. The worker diligently introduced the boy to his mother, securing for him a birthright, namely, the right to know his origins. An outcome fixed firmly in mind, the worker proceeded to work toward reunification and accomplished this in several months. One year later, the mother returned her son to his old foster home, the only home he had known almost from birth. Not unexpectedly, the boy began wildly testing his foster parents, raising questions about whether he could remain there. His school achievements, which had been superior, deteriorated, and he began fighting with peers, particularly with a foster brother placed during his absence. This is surely a case in which the proverbial path to hell was paved by good intentions badly understood and implemented.

Driven by a need to document and account for its results, social work has become obsessed with outcome at the expense of process. Social workers too readily yield proud traditions of respect for self-determination and diverse problem-solving and join, both as victims and collaborators, with those who would manage exclusively by objectives. Life is far more complex than such oversimplified notions. Outcomes are important, but not at the expense of process and sense.

An encouraging trend is that social workers are beginning to distinguish carefully between deviance and difference, a critical distinction in determining how to help people use their inherent strengths to help themselves. "It is becoming increasingly clear that one person's trauma may be another's triumph."[15] There is also evidence that professional social work is learning how to link effectively with self-help groups, reducing professional parochialism and insularity. However, it is important now not to idealize the self-help groups, which the profession earlier viewed nervously as a threat. Some self-help groups have become cults and turned to styles that value conformity and obedience over autonomy and choice.

The profession is learning to distinguish the kinds of life stresses that disrupt human functioning, and various methods to address loss, grief, divorce, and separations seem to be evolving. Here, too, the need to differentiate a general condition from true proximal causes must be recognized.

Social workers are increasingly recognizing that professing firm adherence to a specific field of practice and extolling the features that distinguish each brand of practice from its rivals impedes the necessary work of acknowledging and utilizing commonalities which can profitably enrich all practice.[16] Siporin comments that in spite of discord, social workers have made advances in recent years in achieving "a new strong paradigm of practice . . . at a basic profession wide level."[17] To support this contention, he cites the work of numerous authors, including Brill, Goldstein, Lowenberg, and Minahan.

On another point, Siporin wisely notes that how workers describe their work does not invariably match the reality of their interventions.[18] This is not necessarily a charge about worker dishonesty, although selective accounting sometimes favors hopes more accurately than actions. In fact, practice involves a participant-observer who actively engaged in the work; the work must usually be reconstructed later, a process that is open to distortion and selection, to say nothing of the vast differences even among practitioners of the same faith.

When others not engaged in practice have described and reconstructed social work activities, the accuracy is not improved. Researchers—those members of the field credited with the most objective and scientific stance—are as hampered by methodological impurities and imperfections as those engaged in practice. As the halo fades that the profession defensively and ambivalently accorded its researchers, opportunities open for a new and productive realignment between practice and research methodologies.

One final consideration in any assessment of social work methods is the matter of professional self-perception and need. We social workers meet daily the harshest of human conditions. These can and do blunt our ability to assess with patience and care the needs of those who seek our help. We cannot respond perceptively and appropriately unless we win for ourselves the conditions in which to find renewal and hope. Many of us work in settings that provide no such opportunities. Burned-out workers cannot impart hope to burned-out clients. Recent work on narcissism teaches us to find ways to help clients reassert some modicum of self-esteem.[19] So too, must we, as a profession, seek the conditions and rights necessary to practice with competence and confidence.

Notes and References

1. Jerome D. Frank, "Mental Health in a Fragmented Society: The Shattered Crystal Ball," *American Journal of Orthopsychiatry*, 49 (July 1979), p. 402.

2. *See* Marc Pilisuk, "Scarcity in Human Resources," *American Journal of Orthopsychiatry*, 50 (April 1980), p. 203.

3. Margaret Galdston Frank, "Boundaries of Theory and Practice," *American Journal of Orthopsychiatry*, 49 (July 1979), p. 305.

4. Urie Bronfenbrenner, "Origins of Alienation," *Scientific American*, 231(1974), p. 53.

5. *San Francisco Chronicle*, October 21, 1979.

6. Annabel Teberg, paper delivered at the Annual Convention of the American Academy of Pediatrics, San Francisco, Calif., October 14, 1979.

7. Max Siporin, "Practice Theory for Clinical Social Workers," *Clinical Social Work Journal*, 7 (Summer 1979), p. 76.

8. Carol Meyer, "What Directions for Direct Practice?" *Social Work,* 24 (July 1979), p. 268.

9. Shirley Cooper, "Reflections on Clinical Social Work," in Mary L. Gottesfeld and Helen Pinkus, eds., *Education for Clinical Social Work* (New York: Human Sciences Press, 1977), pp. 303–315.

10. Meyer, op. cit., pp. 269–270.

11. *See,* for example, Carel Germain, "An Ecological Perspective in Casework Practice," *Social Casework* 54 (1973), pp. 323–333.

12. Shirley Cooper, "Social Work: A Dissenting Profession," *Social Work,* 22 (September 1977), pp. 360–367.

13. Selma Fraiberg, "Depressed Teenage Mothers and Their Malattached Infants." Paper presented at the Annual Convention of the American Academy of Pediatrics, San Francisco, October 1979.

14. *See,* for example, Sandra L. Holman, "An Early Intervention Program for Developmentally At-Risk Toddlers and Their Mothers," *Clinical Social Work Journal,* 7 (Fall 1979), pp. 167–181; and Helen Reid et al., paper presented at the Annual Meeting of the American Orthopsychiatric Association, New York, 1973.

15. Shirley Cooper, "Reflections on the Mental Health System," *American Journal of Orthopsychiatry,* 46 (July 1976), p. 394.

16. Jerome D. Frank, op. cit., p. 403.

17. Siporin, op. cit., p. 77.

18. Ibid.

19. *See,* for example, Joseph Palombo, "Theories of Narcissism and the Practice of Clinical Social Work," *Clinical Social Work Journal,* 4 (Fall 1976), pp. 147–161.

Notes

Notes

Notes

2M/Pubs./11/80